"Get ready to dive headfirst into this cookbook! Yumna's recipes are made with feel-good ingredients and with fewer than ten ingredients, plus her book is packed with practical advice in the kitchen."

—**GINA HOMOLKA,** *New York Times* bestselling author of *The Skinnytaste Cookbook*

"True to Yumna's reputation, her cookbook is filled with mouthwatering recipes that will make you hungry, get you excited about cooking, and make you *feel good*! One look at the ingredients, the simple steps, and the beautiful photography and you'll want to roll up your sleeves and dive into Mediterranean cuisine."

—**NATASHA KRAVCHUK,** *New York Times* bestselling author of *Natasha's Kitchen*

"Yumna's debut cookbook knocks it out of the park and highlights the vibrant, feel-good foods that she's known for (and loved for!) across social media. I'm such a fan of Mediterranean and Middle Eastern–infused flavor, and with how delicious these recipes are, I know you'll go back to this cookbook time and again!"

—**LISA BRYAN,** bestselling author of *Downshiftology Healthy Meal Prep*

"My girl Yumna is my go-to foodie when I want easy-to-follow Mediterranean recipes that are family friendly. She knows how to keep it simple enough for busy weeknights without compromising on flavor, and it's food I feel good about eating and serving!"

—**MY NGUYEN,** author and creator of *My Healthy Dish*

"How exciting that followers of *Feel Good Foodie* who appreciate Yumna's simple recipes and kitchen hacks now have her in print! I know this book will be treasured by many. Congratulations, Yumna!"

—**SUZY KARADSHEH,** *New York Times* bestselling author and founder of *The Mediterranean Dish*

"Yumna hits the Mediterranean flavors out of the park in her debut cookbook! If you're not already stocking your pantry with zaatar and labneh, start adding them to your weekly shopping list, because you'll find an incredible amount of recipes in this book that you'll be wanting to work into your weekly rotation. From Roasted Garlic Sumac Bread to Crispy Feta Greek Salad with Zaatar Vinaigrette to a White Zucchini Pizza, consider me totally obsessed!"

—**GABY DALKIN,** *New York Times* bestselling author and creator of *What's Gaby Cooking*

THE
feel good foodie
COOKBOOK

THE
feel good foodie
COOKBOOK

125 RECIPES Enhanced with
Mediterranean Flavors

YUMNA JAWAD

with Julia Clancy

RODALE
NEW YORK

Library of Congress Cataloging-in-Publication Data
Names: Jawad, Yumna, author. | Clancy, Julia (Food writer),
    author.
Title: The feel good foodie cookbook / Yumna Jawad with Julia
    Clancy.
Description: First edition. | New York : Rodale [2024] | Includes
    index.
Identifiers: LCCN 2023018501 (print) | LCCN 2023018502
    (ebook) | ISBN 9780593579503 (hardcover) | ISBN
    9780593579510 (ebook)
Subjects: LCSH: Cooking, Mediterranean. | Quick and easy
    cooking. | LCGFT: Cookbooks.
Classification: LCC TX725.M35 J39 2024 (print) | LCC TX725.
    M35 (ebook) | DDC 641.59/1822--dc23/eng/20230424
LC record available at https://lccn.loc.gov/2023018501
LC ebook record available at https://lccn.loc.gov/2023018502

ISBN 978-0-593-57950-3
Ebook ISBN 978-0-593-57951-0

Printed in China

Design by Rae Ann Spitzenberger
Photographs by Doaa Elkady

10 9 8 7 6 5 4 3 2 1

First Edition

To Carine and Adam:
here's to whipping up endless
delicious moments together
in the kitchen—a recipe for
lifelong laughter and love

Contents

Introduction

I saw my mom cook for a family of six growing up—it looked hard and tiring. There was so much to learn and so many things to accidentally burn! Even though I loved to eat and was deeply curious about food as a child, I figured I was safer out of my mom's way, helping set the table and do the dishes. Then I went from having zero kitchen skills to cooking for millions of followers online. But it didn't happen overnight.

My family is originally from Lebanon and, until I was eleven years old, I grew up in a predominantly Lebanese community in the small West African country of Sierra Leone. I can't remember a single restaurant in the tiny town we lived in, and there were only a couple of small grocery stores. I didn't grow up ordering pizzas or eating ready-to-heat enchiladas. My mom prepared virtually every meal from scratch with Mediterranean ingredients seven days a week. It wasn't trendy. It was just what we ate.

Walking into our bright, blue-tiled kitchen in Sierra Leone always felt like entering a mom-and-pop café—it was small, cozy, and always smelled like there was something good cooking. I can time travel to that kitchen so easily in my mind because, in retrospect, I think I was learning to cook from the earliest days of childhood—I just began learning through listening and observing. There were the clang of pots and pans, the thunk of Mom chopping fresh vegetables, and the hiss of onions meeting hot fat. Unforgettable aromas sifted through that space, like cardamom blooming in melted butter or garlic and cilantro sizzling in the hot, overworked skillet. I remember how my mom's fingers delicately and confidently stuffed small squashes with fragrant rice and ground beef, and how she would whisper a quiet prayer every time she transferred something hot, like just-made yogurt, into a big bowl. Most of the time, our meals weren't complicated. Maybe dinner would be Lemony Grilled Chicken Kabobs (page 205) marinated in olive oil, lemon, and garlic and then grilled outside over smoking charcoal—we ate that with Tabbouleh Salad (page 102), which was mounded with fresh herbs that perfumed the whole kitchen when they were minced. Or maybe we'd enjoy warm bowls of Crushed Lentil Soup (page 148), which could spend an entire day simmering on the back burner. My mom's meals didn't just feed our bodies and souls. They made us feel good.

When I turned eleven, in 1993, my parents made the difficult decision to leave Sierra Leone due to the political climate. We moved to the United States to live in Dearborn, Michigan— the largest Lebanese community outside of Lebanon—where my father had many relatives. And the grocery stores in the American Midwest? *Wow!* The shelves looked quite a bit different from those in my little town back home in Africa! Shopping for food with my mom, I could feel the fireworks going off in her brain: *Oh my gosh, I can buy Tuna Helper and have dinner on the table in seven minutes!* But instead of zeroing in on packaged foods over scratch-made foods or vice versa, my mom figured out how to use convenience foods to create shortcuts for her more traditional Mediterranean recipes.

A can of tomato paste, for instance, could save hours of simmering down fresh tomatoes but still deliver the same rich flavor in stews. Buying a ready-made tub of yogurt—which is used for so many condiments, sauces, and marinades in Mediterranean recipes—would save the labor-intensive process of heating fresh milk, transferring it from one pot to the other, and checking it throughout the day until it reached the desired consistency. Mom embraced frozen vegetables, store-bought vegetable broth, and canned chickpeas. She also cleverly figured out how to use some of her favorite Mediterranean ingredients to enhance the American dishes we liked in the Midwest, adding cumin- and cinnamon-flecked seven spice to marinara sauce and hamburger patties or stirring toasty, nutty tahini into Sesame Banana Bread (page 48). With these thoughtfully chosen, time-saving tweaks, her usual repertoire of homemade meals suddenly took about as much time as a box of Rice-A-Roni—all while maintaining her delicious and satisfying results. And though my mom's kitchen in Michigan was thousands of miles from the one we had left in Africa, I was still hit

> ## The way I love to cook revolves around unfussy, nutrient-dense, back-pocket meals that infuse my Mediterranean upbringing with my new Midwestern roots.

daily by the comforting, familiar fragrances of childhood, like garlic, sumac, parsley, rose water, and lemons.

I bet you're thinking this is the part where I tell you I quickly became a cooking pro, that all those hours listening and observing as my mom made her Mediterranean masterpieces meant I could finally pick up a knife and let loose. Nope! At times, my mom would put me to work arranging fruits on platters for guests or squeezing more lemon juice into her fresh batch of hummus. That was pretty much it. (We did eventually realize that as a rather ambitious, *detail-oriented* person, I was well suited to take on the delicate task of rolling stuffed grape leaves.) Truth be told, I didn't really start cooking until I got married.

In my first year of marriage, I was working full-time at a corporate job, my husband was busy with medical school, and I found myself with almost no hands-on cooking knowledge in my wheelhouse. Why learn to cook when I could be spoiled by my mother, who was a *great* cook? (In those early days of marriage, I would drive by my mom's house on my way home from work and pick up dinner—seriously, it was like my very own personal take-out service!) Eventually, I was determined to give my growing family the comfort of home-cooked Mediterranean meals that my mom gave us growing up. So, one phone

call at a time, I asked her to teach me my favorite dishes, starting with the most basic recipe I could think of: Vermicelli Rice (page 224).

With that first dish in my repertoire, I slowly started gathering the tools to learn more. I turned to the Internet, both to absorb as much information as possible and to start building a two-way conversation with a virtual network of cooks and food lovers. I documented my progress on Instagram under the name Feel Good Foodie and, in the meantime, accidentally inspired strangers—millions of strangers from all over the world—to cook, too. We created a community of cooks and eaters that included tired parents, aspirational home cooks, enthusiastic grocery shoppers, and feel-good ingredient seekers, all with good appetites. This community of new and seasoned cooks alike saw my recipe fails, tweaks, and triumphs. Most importantly, cooks everywhere saw themselves in me.

Today, the way I love to cook and feed my family revolves around unfussy, nutrient-dense, back-pocket meals that infuse my Mediterranean upbringing with my new Midwestern roots. The recipes in this cookbook also showcase the eight superstar ingredients that are always in my fridge and pantry: seven spice, pomegranate molasses, rose water, sumac, tahini, zaatar, dates, and labneh. (Read more about them on page 16.) These eight staples, which enhance tons of recipes throughout this book, are what charge my food with that Mediterranean zing. (They also essentially last forever when stored properly.) They have the sweet, savory, bright, tart, warm, and rich notes that evoke the tastes and smells of my childhood, no matter how they're used. A sprinkle of zaatar on homemade focaccia, for example, adds savory, herby flavor. A generous spoonful of labneh in pancake batter lends moisture, protein, and a satisfying hint of tang. And the smell of sun-warmed rose petals enclosed in a bottle of rose water is a subtle but intoxicating reminder of

home every time the infusion sparingly dropped into a bowl of fruit salad.

In this cookbook, you'll find 125 simple recipes for Mediterranean-inspired meals, plus tons of handy tips to get you from breakfast through dessert, with everything in between. As a mom of two who hates food waste and loves a good budget, I even included a section before the recipes dedicated to making leftovers shine (see What to Do with Leftovers on page 32). And because these are the same dishes I cook for my own family and friends, trust me when I tell you that I'm not going to share a recipe with you unless I know it can check all these boxes:

1 **It's going to take thirty minutes or less of active cooking time.** Okay, so there is one exception to this rule: falafel (forty minutes of active time). That's because this traditional Lebanese dish simply isn't as good with shortcuts—believe me, I've tried! Trust me: if it wasn't the best Crispy Falafel (page 156), it wouldn't be in this book.

2 **It includes ingredients you can find at your local supermarket or easily source online.** (But don't forget about your local Middle Eastern grocer!)

3 **It has at least one "feel good" ingredient,** such as fruits, veggies, grains, or legumes, and highlights diverse ways to use some of my favorite Mediterranean staples.

4 **It calls for fewer than ten ingredients,** not including the usual suspects of olive oil, salt, and pepper. Now, a caveat: Out of 125 recipes, there are just a few very special exceptions to this rule. Instead of toggling with these recipes, most of which are special-to-me Lebanese classics, I decided to keep them as is because they're truly worth the extra one or two ingredients.

5 **It works!** Whether it's Toum (page 261), endlessly customizable My Four Favorite Overnight Oats (page 39), or my Baked Feta Pasta (page 159—this one went viral online with more than thirty million views), I am always going to give you a recipe that's thoroughly tested and that even the most novice cook can nail in the kitchen.

At the end of the day, this book is meant to make you *feel good*—whether that's because you're cooking and eating homemade food, you're finally feeling confident in your kitchen, or you're making dishes that you and your people love. I wasn't born with the special ability to look at a fridge full of ingredients and execute their delicious, nutritious potential. (Who is?) But with an open mind, hours of phone calls with my mom, and lots of practice, I was able to start cooking for myself and my family the way I always knew I wanted to, all while honoring my Mediterranean home base. I know you can get there, too, no calls with my mom required (even though she'd happily say hello!). I promise if you bring your own open mind and a sense of adventure, I can equip you with the tools for working your own magic in the kitchen. So, how about we find something good to cook?

My Eight Mediterranean Staples

The recipes in this book are simple, but each one has something special that makes people say, "Wow! What's in that recipe?" They might love that unexpected hit of lemon zest, mint, or cardamom, but most of the time this "wow" factor is thanks to a thoughtful use of one of my eight favorite ingredients. These ingredients are heroes in my kitchen because they have the power to give ordinary recipes a unique and pleasantly surprising spin that tastes *so good*! As you cook your way through this book, I think you'll learn to love them as much as I do.

These staples in my kitchen (and in my recipes) are not only powerhouses of Mediterranean flavor and texture—they're also easy to use and, when stored properly, keep for months. What's not to love? You can find all eight ingredients online, at many supermarkets, or at any Middle Eastern grocer. Some of them you can even make at home, like Labneh (page 258).

SEVEN SPICE

Every cook has a different spin on this traditional Levantine spice blend. Warming, fragrant, sweet, and savory, seven spice— also called *sabaa baharat*, which means "seven spices" in Arabic—is so crucial to the Mediterranean kitchen. I seriously think this is the one spice blend my mom cannot live without. It's a must-have in traditional dishes like Tahini Kafta (page 214) and Hashweh (page 217). It's also the perfect way to infuse a modern Mediterranean take on virtually any dish in my kitchen—try a pinch in a pot of rice or a crispy grilled cheese. Yes, you can buy it premade, but it's also a cinch to make at home (see page 259). My blend has the perfect balance of cinnamon, allspice, black pepper, cloves, coriander, cumin, and nutmeg.

POMEGRANATE MOLASSES

Pomegranate molasses is made by boiling fresh pomegranate juice until it thickens and transforms into a sticky (like, seriously sticky), tart, floral, and sweet syrup that enhances everything it touches. It's kind of like the Eastern Mediterranean version of balsamic glaze. As you make your way through this book, you'll see just how versatile pomegranate molasses can be. It's integral to the dressing for Mama's Fattoush Salad (page 101), but I also stir it into Chocolate Pomegranate Overnight Oats (page 39), use it as a sticky-savory marinade for Mediterranean-Style BBQ Flank Steak (page 221), drizzle it over Caramelized Eggplant with Mint Yogurt (page 93), and let it lend my Pomegranate Green Bean Salad (page 123) a sweet-tart depth of flavor. That's just the start for this magic ingredient!

ROSE WATER

Rose water is sneakily fabulous despite its simplicity. It's made by steeping rose petals in fresh water until the essence of the flower is transformed into a pourable liquid. A shelf-stable bottle of rose water can literally last for years because a mere drop added to a dish goes a long way. It's used in a wide range of Mediterranean cooking, from Rose Water Fruit Salad (page 250; my mom's favorite way to use it) to Strawberry Rose Pancakes (page 44) to Rose-Mango Rice Pudding (page 273) to the most amazing Raspberry Rose Fro-Yo (page 274). Rose water can seem a bit strong if it's your first time trying it, so it's worth going slowly when adding it to your recipes and tasting as you go. You want a *subtle* hint!

SUMAC

Sumac is a reddish-purple spice made from the finely ground berries of the sumac shrubs native to rocky Mediterranean climates. Its warm, pungent, and tart-lemon taste makes it very dynamic. Sumac is a key way to add a punch of flavor and brightness to any Mediterranean meal without using extra liquid like vinegar or lemon juice. That's a win-win for any dish in my book, from Roasted Garlic Sumac Bread (page 75) to Cast-Iron Sumac Chicken (page 209) to Sumac Sweet Potato Wedges (page 229). Sumac is used frequently in spice blends like zaatar, but it also stands alone as one of my go-to methods for lending bright, tart flavor to sweet or savory recipes.

TAHINI

I like to call tahini the peanut butter of the Middle East. It's made from toasted hulled sesame seeds that are ground until smooth, creamy, and spreadable. I prefer storing tahini upside down in my pantry—it keeps the texture pourable, which is necessary because I go through it so fast. Tahini is one of the best ways to boost any dish with richness and flavor. You might already be familiar with tahini in things like hummus and salad dressings, but when it comes to this magical ingredient, there's so much more you can do! It makes many, many cameos in almost every chapter of this book, from Tahini Caesar Salad (page 98) to Apricot Cardamom Granola (page 249) to Not My Baba's Ghanoush (page 67). And feel free to explore: Try spooning tahini into a soup or stew to add more body and richness. Slather it over chicken and vegetables before roasting to lock in natural moisture and make everything even more

caramelized and juicy. Or use tahini in sweets like Sesame Banana Bread (page 48), Mixed Berry Sumac Crisp (page 278), and the best Banana Tahini Shake (page 286) for a hint of toasty, nutty flavor!

ZAATAR

Zaatar is one of the most widely used spice blends in the Mediterranean kitchen. It's my number one flavor companion, so you'll find it at all times in a thirty-two-ounce jar in my fridge instead of in my spice drawer (there's not enough room!). The mix itself can differ from region to region, but I'm naturally biased toward the Lebanese zaatar that my family brings me in bulk from our village in Lebanon. The blend I use in these recipes is a strong, bright, herby mix of sumac, dried thyme, sesame seeds, and salt. Growing up in the Midwest, my mom would sprinkle zaatar on pita with labneh, and the kids at school would joke that it looked like I was eating dirt. Ah, middle school! But I loved it so much I just embraced their jokes and kept asking for it in my lunch box. Now, zaatar remains a key ingredient in making pita and labneh sandwiches for my own kids, and it stays front-and-center in many of my recipes, such as Zaatar Manakeesh (page 43), Zaatar Focaccia (page 72), and my Crispy Feta Greek Salad with Zaatar Vinaigrette (page 115).

DATES

Dates are nature's energy bites. They have a caramel-like flavor and almost fudgy texture, and it never fails to delight me that candy can grow on trees. Dates grow in large clusters on date palms, a type of tree that's native to the Middle East and has been a central player in regional Mediterranean cooking for thousands of years. Dates are also packed with fiber, vitamins, minerals, and natural sugars, making them an ideal way to break my fast during the month of Ramadan. Aside from that, I always have dates on hand for adding to things like Pecan Date Bars (page 246), my favorite Mint Chocolate Smoothie (page 60), Couscous-Almond Pilaf with Dates (page 230), and Brownie Date Balls (page 243). Medjool dates are my go-to for their large, soft texture and cinnamon-toffee flavor, and they're the dates I use in this cookbook.

LABNEH

Labneh is like an extra-smooth, spreadable Mediterranean cream cheese. It's made by straining yogurt to remove most of its whey, resulting in a thick, tangy, creamy, and supremely delicious cultured dairy product. You can find labneh in most grocery stores, but it's actually quite simple to make at home (page 258) if you have a little extra time. I love slathering labneh on Arabic-style pita with a pile of fresh herbs in my Scrambled Eggs & Labneh Pita (page 52), mixing it into the perfect dip for my Crispy Cauliflower with Mint-Avocado Crema (page 85), or using it as a secret flavor boost in my Roasted Tomato Soup with Labneh (page 140). You'll also see the phrase "Labneh, for serving" quite a few times throughout this book!

Kitchen Essentials

You know that feeling when you open and close your pantry, then open and close your fridge, then open both again, and you're still not sure what to make? Yup, me, too! And because I really love to eat, I learned over time to bridge the gap between thinking about what I wanted to eat and being able to bring whatever it was to life. In my kitchen, cooking starts with knowing how to stock the essentials.

Having an answer to "What's in my fridge?" (or pantry or spice cabinet) makes everyday cooking—when I'm short on time, short on inspiration, balancing carpools, or just plain tired—much simpler. Here's a tour of my kitchen and how I keep it stocked and ready to go.

WHAT'S IN MY FRIDGE?

Milk: I like 2% cow's milk, and that's what I use in most of these recipes. But unless otherwise noted, feel free to use whatever milk you have or prefer.

Plant-Based Milk: I alternate between almond, oat, and cashew milks for things like smoothies and overnight oats.

Cheeses: I have an entire fridge drawer dedicated to cheese! My preferences change with my mood and the weather, and I'll often rotate between three different cheeses at a time. I always stock a couple of semisoft cheeses such as Havarti, Gouda, or mozzarella; halloumi, a great semihard cheese for grilling and searing; a hard cheese like aged Parmesan; soft, spreadable cheeses like Boursin, cream cheese, or The Laughing Cow; sticks and cubes of snacking cheeses for my two kids (they love mozzarella and Cheddar); and, of course, my favorite flavor multitasker: feta.

Cultured Dairy: Thanks to my Mediterranean upbringing, I also have an entire cultured dairy section in my fridge. This includes Greek yogurt, plain yogurt, cottage cheese, ricotta, sour cream, and labneh, all of which are great for bulking up recipes with an added dose of protein and flavor.

Butter: I like to use salted butter in most of my savory cooking (and for spreading on toast!) and unsalted butter for most of my baking. (Generally, it won't make a big difference if you swap one for the other, though if you're using salted butter in baked goods or sweet recipes, just remember not to add the extra salt listed in the recipe itself—you won't need it.) If you find yourself with too much butter on hand (is there such a thing?), you can store it in blocks or sticks in the freezer for up to a year.

Fresh Fruits: I always have a mix of fresh berries (such as strawberries, raspberries, and blueberries) and a large bunch of grapes in my fridge. Here's how I store them as soon as I get home from the store: First, I soak them in water and a teaspoon of white vinegar for about a minute, which helps remove any surface dirt and makes the fruits last longer (you don't taste the vinegar!). Next, I drain them in a colander and store them in clear, ventilated containers lined with a layer of paper towels at the bottom to soak up any excess moisture. I also like to have some cut-up cantaloupe, pineapple, or watermelon— because I've learned if it's not already cut into pieces, nobody in my house will eat it.

Fresh Vegetables: I always have celery, carrots, cucumbers, avocados, and bell peppers on hand for quick dinner inspiration, since these vegetables can be the base of so many meals. In my crisper drawers, I'll store a couple of cruciferous vegetables (such as cabbage, cauliflower, and broccoli), some romaine lettuce or mixed greens for quick salads, and some dark leafy greens, such as kale and spinach.

Fresh Herbs: Fresh herbs are crucial to the Mediterranean kitchen, and I always have a few mixed bunches. My core herbs are mint, parsley, basil, and cilantro, which I keep stored in the fridge like a bouquet of flowers in a mason jar filled with water (this keeps them fresh and perky for about two weeks). The exception is basil, which tends to wilt too quickly—instead, I'll lay the leaves flat in a single layer on some paper towels, roll the paper towel around the leaves (kind of like I'm making a sandwich wrap), and store it in the crisper drawer in a tightly sealed storage bag.

Eggs: I usually have two dozen eggs on hand for easy meals and bursts of baking energy. I use large pasture-raised eggs in my kitchen and in the recipes in this cookbook.

Condiments: Olives punch way above their weight in the flavor department. I like to have two or three varieties on hand to choose from, including meaty green olives (such as Castelvetrano or Cerignola), Kalamata olives, and oil-cured black olives. My fridge also packs all of the pickles, like Pickled Turnips (page 252), Pickled Red Onions (page 253), sliced dill pickles, cornichons, capers, and banana peppers. My condiments shelf also has sun-dried tomatoes, roasted red peppers, ketchup, yellow mustard, Dijon mustard, mayonnaise, hot sauce, Worcestershire sauce, maple syrup, and a few types of jam. I also keep zaatar in the fridge because I purchase it in two-pound bags from Lebanon—it gets transferred into a giant mason jar in the fridge because it lasts longer at the cooler temperature. If you don't buy zaatar in bulk like me, though, it will be just fine in your pantry.

Baking Soda: A box of baking soda in the fridge neutralizes food odors, so I always keep mine stashed in there—and, win-win, it still works great when I pull it out for baking.

WHAT'S IN MY FREEZER?

Fruits and Vegetables: Frozen fruits and vegetables have the same (and sometimes more) nutrients as their fresh counterparts. (Google it!) And they're such a great hack for busy people. They make it easier for me and my family to eat enough fruits and vegetables throughout the week, and they also ensure that my produce is frozen at peak freshness.

For frozen fruits, which I love for smoothies and baking, I always have sliced (and peeled, if necessary) leftover fruits that were on the verge of overripening, like peaches, bananas, strawberries, and any less-than-perky berries. I also buy frozen mango and a frozen berry medley at the supermarket when fresh is unavailable or out of season.

For frozen vegetables, my superstars are peas, green beans, corn, and spinach—since they're already shelled, stemmed, or cooked, they make getting meals on the table so much simpler. I use them to make stews like Healing Couscous Chicken Soup (page 147), or sometimes I just sauté them straight from the freezer with some olive oil, salt, and pepper for a quick side dish. Seriously, I love frozen vegetables! Nothing adds a dose of color or nutrients to a meal faster.

Freezer Scrap Bag: This big old bag in the freezer is my trick for infusing soups, stocks, and stews with flavor, all while minimizing food waste and stretching my dollar further. This

Easy Scratch-Made Stock

▶▶▶ Want to know the easiest way to make stock from scratch? Cover the contents of a freezer scrap bag with 2 inches of water in a large pot and bring to a boil. (Sometimes, but not always, I'll add a couple of bay leaves or a few meaty bones for good measure.) Reduce the heat to medium-low and simmer, uncovered, for 50 minutes. Strain the liquid and discard the solids. Now you have a pretty fantastic homemade stock. Magic! Use it immediately for soups and stews, or let it cool to room temperature and freeze, tightly sealed, for up to 3 months.

scrap bag gets all my carrot peels, onion peels, celery leaves, and herb stems. I honestly throw almost any clean produce scraps in there, except for cruciferous vegetables (which make broths astringent) or fennel fronds (which are flavorful enough to make everything taste like fennel).

Meat: I only buy halal meat, and one of the best places to source it is back home in Dearborn, Michigan, which has a large Muslim community. I try to buy a three-month supply and get a variety of types to store in the freezer, from usual suspects like chicken thighs and breasts to more specific cuts like drumsticks, flank steak, or shawarma (thinly shaved slices of steak that I always freeze flat). At the beginning of each week, I'll transfer a couple of frozen meats to a large paper towel–lined plate in the fridge to thaw for a day or two before cooking. Ground beef often features in that rotation—cooked in a skillet over medium heat with olive oil and a tablespoon of seven spice (see my recipe for Hashweh, page 217), it's a great head start for so many easy meals.

Seafood: I'll buy seafood anywhere since it doesn't have to be halal, but I prefer wild-caught. I usually have shrimp, cod, and salmon

in my freezer for easy, any-season dinners, but occasionally I like to diversify with tuna, flounder, halibut, or regional catches I want my family to try. And here's an important tip specific to seafood, if you mostly purchase it frozen like me: Before thawing, remove the seafood from its packaging and transfer it to a covered bowl or glass storage container. *Then* transfer it to the fridge the night before cooking. This simple move allows air to circulate and inhibits potential bacterial growth as it thaws.

Ginger and Turmeric: I freeze whole "hands" and "thumbs" of ginger and turmeric. I don't peel them first because the skin is edible; I just make sure to give them a good scrub and dry first so they're clean going into the freezer. They last pretty much forever, and they're actually easier to grate when frozen (and in terms of bright orange turmeric, less prone to staining your tools and cutting boards). I use ginger and turmeric in soups and stir-fries and even for making tea!

Garlic: Every three months or so, I put about six cups of peeled garlic cloves in a food processor and pulse them to a chunky paste. I put this garlic paste in a resealable snack bag (six cups will make around six to eight snack bags), lay the bags flat, and, using the dull back side of a knife, press the garlic paste into portioned one-inch squares (around a teaspoon each). I freeze the bags flat until solid, and then stack the bags in the freezer. Now I can just unzip the bags and slice or break off as many squares as I need for any cooked recipes. I use my frozen garlic stash almost daily, except for the recipes (such as hummus and salad dressings) where the fresh taste of raw garlic is necessary.

Bulk Nuts: If I have more nuts than my family and I can eat in a month, I store the extras in the freezer. This is especially true for pine nuts, which I only really use for making pesto or special Lebanese dishes, like Spaghetti with

Garlicky Yogurt Sauce (page 163) and Hashweh (page 217). Nuts can go rancid, losing their crunchy texture and gaining a bitter aftertaste. Storing them in the freezer prolongs their shelf life up to a year.

Ice Cream and Frozen Pizza: Because is a freezer considered fully stocked without them?

WHAT'S IN MY PANTRY

Grains and Pastas: I always stock long-grain basmati rice for traditional Middle Eastern recipes, as well as short-grain rice for stuffed recipes (like stuffed grape leaves and stuffed peppers). Every once in a while, I'll buy brown rice or wild rice, just to have some variety. A few of my other favorite grains include couscous, bulgur, farro, freekeh, and barley. My must-have pastas are spaghetti, lasagna noodles, and elbow macaroni, but I love buying different shapes and sizes for variety—like bow-tie pasta, which seriously doesn't get the good reputation it deserves! Of course, let's not forget oats, including steel-cut oats for heartier breakfasts, rolled oats for daily oatmeal, and quick-cooking oats for recipes like my No-Bake Oat Bites (page 243).

Baking Ingredients: I have a ten-pound jar of all-purpose flour that I use for all my baking needs. Sometimes, though, I'll experiment with things like gluten-free flour blends and almond flour (which I think adds nice structure to no-bake desserts). I also keep white sugar, brown sugar, maple syrup, honey, and Medjool dates on hand, as well as nut and seed butters like peanut butter and tahini. And my pantry wouldn't be complete without a bottle of rose water.

Legumes: Green lentils and red lentils are my go-to for so many Middle Eastern recipes, like Mujadara (page 167) and Crushed Lentil Soup (page 148). Sometimes I imagine myself to be the type of person who soaks beans the night before cooking, but listen, aside from my (ahem, amazing) Crispy Falafel (page 156), if I'm craving beans, it's the canned kind I'm reaching for 90 percent of the time. They're so easy, quick, and tasty! I love canned black beans, white beans, and chickpeas, and my pantry is never without them.

Oils and Vinegars: For the most part, I rotate between five kinds of oil. I use olive oil for high-heat cooking and extra-virgin olive oil for almost everything else. Avocado oil is for shallow- or deep-frying, since it has such a high smoke point, and for recipes where a neutral-tasting oil works best. I use coconut oil for some baked goods (particularly vegan treats) and organic canola oil exclusively for two recipes: Toum (page 261) and Crispy Falafel (page 156). Red wine vinegar and balsamic vinegar are my favorites, but distilled white vinegar has to be on hand for Mama's Beef Shawarma (page 213).

Salty Snacks: Bulk nuts and seeds are for the freezer, but anything outside of a big old bag gets stashed in the pantry: almonds, cashews, pine nuts, and sesame seeds are the ones I go for most often. I also like to have a few different kinds of crackers (remember how I have a whole fridge drawer dedicated to cheese?) plus seaweed snacks, popcorn, pretzels, and tortilla chips.

Sweet Snacks: Fruit snacks and granola bars are some of the easiest snacks for kids and adults alike, and sometimes I'll even make a homemade batch of granola for easy breakfasts on weekday mornings (try my Apricot Cardamom Granola on page 249). I own a company called Oath that specializes in naturally sweetened granola, overnight oats, and oat bars, so you know my pantry is well represented in that arena, too! I also always have chocolate, which is self-explanatory.

Arabic Foods: Aside from some previously mentioned Mediterranean staples like tahini, dates, rose water, and lentils, my must-have Arabic ingredient is vermicelli, a type of pasta that's thin and usually comes broken into one-inch pieces. And no Mediterranean pantry is complete without a solid stash of spices, which always taste fresh since we go through them so frequently. (Which reminds me: if you've been hanging onto a spice for more than two years, it has probably lost most of its pungency and flavor. My advice is to only buy what you need and replenish your spice drawer annually.) The spices I use the most are sumac, zaatar, Seven Spice (page 259), garlic powder, dried mint, dried thyme, turmeric, cinnamon, and cardamom.

Other Canned Goods: Year-round, I will always have canned tomatoes of every kind: sauce, paste, diced, crushed, and whole-peeled. I can't imagine my pantry without them! I also keep full-fat, unsweetened canned coconut milk for a few cooking and baking recipes. And a few cans of tuna never hurt, either, especially for last-minute dinners like my Lemon-Dill Tuna Patties (page 197).

Dry-Storage Produce: My pantry is an allium and potato party since I use these ingredients so often. I always have red onions, sweet onions, and yellow onions, plus shallots, garlic, sweet potatoes, and white potatoes. And I lose sleep if I don't have at least ten lemons and limes readily available.

WHAT'S IN MY CABINET?

I keep it simple with my kitchen tools and gadgets, but my cabinets have a few workhorses that I really can't live without. Some of these things might be must-haves for you, too, or maybe they're purchases to keep in mind for the future. The key is to thoughtfully invest in a few small and large pieces of equipment that help maximize flavor and minimize active time in the kitchen—because, although I love to cook, I'm much more likely to roll up my sleeves in the kitchen when the meal feels simple, delicious, and hard to mess up.

Small Things

Vegetable Peeler: I use a swivel peeler or a Y-peeler, which are both handy for peeling potatoes and carrots or for making ribbons out of zucchini.

Meat Thermometer: I love taking the guesswork out of things. If you're new to cooking meat, a thermometer is especially nice to have on hand for checking internal temperatures for doneness.

Garlic Press: We eat so much garlic in this house, so it's nice to have a tool that shortcuts any chopping and mincing.

Microplane Zester: There are few quicker ways to build depth and flavor in a dish than by adding finely grated fresh citrus zest, nutmeg, shallots, or garlic. This zester also doubles as a cheese grater if you're looking to finish a dish off with a shower of fresh Parmesan.

Small Citrus Press and Juicer: Just like the zest, I love adding a squeeze of fresh citrus juice to my meals. I add lemon to salad dressings, finish off soups or seafood dishes with fresh lime, or add citrus juice to my Citrus & Turmeric Cake (page 282). I use a handheld citrus press when the job requires one or two lemons, but I head for my small electric countertop juicer when it comes to recipes that require squeezing fresh citrus by the cup, like my homemade Mint-Basil Lemonade (page 289).

Immersion Blender: A handheld immersion blender is the simplest way to puree hot soups right in the pot. You can also use it to quickly whip cream or blend a large batch of salad dressing.

Electric Hand Mixer: A handheld, plug-in mixer is better than a stand mixer for smaller-batch projects or recipes with shorter mixing times. I'll take out my stand mixer to help me knead bread, but for spending a couple of minutes creaming butter or whipping cream? Hand mixer it is.

Big Things

Stackable Storage Containers: One of the ways to make your kitchen life simpler is by making cleanup easier. Stackable storage containers with tight-fitting lids help your leftovers stay food safe and ready for repurposing (for leftover ideas, see page 32).

Salad Spinner: It's much less expensive to buy whole heads of lettuce and do the washing and drying at home than it is to buy precut, prepackaged greens. So, I try to do the former as much as possible. Cue the salad spinner, which is also great for washing and drying herbs, small vegetables, chickpeas, and leafy greens of any kind. Trust me, there is no better base for delicious salad dressings than crisp, fresh lettuce leaves.

High-Speed Blender: I have had my high-speed blender for ages, and there is nothing I trust more for whipping up big batches of salad dressing, pesto, tomato sauce, pureed soups, and more. Of course, it also takes my smoothie game up a notch.

Food Processor: My large thirteen-cup food processor is indispensable in my kitchen. (If you're wondering what the difference is between a blender and a food processor, a food processor is designed for a wider variety of kitchen tasks, not just blending and pulverizing.) I pull out my food processor for recipes like Baba's Classic Hummus (page 66), No-Bake Walnut Cheesecake (page 281), and my ultra-smooth Toum (page 261), a Lebanese-style garlic sauce.

What to Do with Leftovers

I'm the kind of cook who likes to jump-start my meals for the week. This could mean making a big batch of grains or overnight oats on a Sunday, washing and drying lettuce for salads when I get home from the grocery store, or whipping up some No-Bake Oat Bites (page 243) for the week ahead. I'm also big on leftovers because I'm all about getting the most mileage as I can out of cooking. (And I've made it one of my goals to create as little food waste as possible—no small feat considering I test multiple recipes a day!) There's an art to repurposing meals and ingredients so they never get boring, and I think that's what the home-cooking pros are best at. In that spirit, here are some of my favorite ways to use what you've got.

Leftover Smoothie →
Delicious Overnight Oats

Use 1 cup of leftover smoothie for every ½ cup oats and stir to combine. If you have a little less than 1 cup of smoothie or if you find your smoothie is too thick, you can dilute it with more milk or water as needed. This might look something like: Mix 1 cup leftover smoothie (such as my Triple Berry Yogurt Smoothie, page 60) with ½ cup oats, 1 tablespoon chia seeds or flaxseeds, and a pinch of ground cinnamon. Rest for at least 3 hours or up to overnight in the fridge. Serve with some fresh berries, if you'd like.

Leftover Bread or Focaccia →
Savory Breakfast Casserole

Slice any leftover bread, pita, or focaccia (such as Zaatar Focaccia, page 72) into 1-inch cubes to make about 4 cups total. Mix the cubed bread in a 9 × 13-inch baking dish with 8 beaten eggs, 1 cup milk, 1 bag of thawed frozen spinach, 2 teaspoons sumac, and ½ teaspoon of salt. Cover tightly with aluminum foil and bake at 350°F for 30 minutes. Remove the foil and scatter the casserole with 1 cup of shredded Cheddar cheese. Bake, uncovered, until the cheese is browned and bubbly, about 30 minutes longer.

Leftover Hummus →
Creamy Pasta Sauce

Whisk about ½ cup of leftover hummus (such as Baba's Classic Hummus, page 66) with 3 tablespoons water—pasta water is even better! Toss the hummus mixture with al dente–cooked spaghetti or linguine in a large skillet over medium heat until warmed through. Add 2 big handfuls of fresh spinach, ¼ teaspoon each of salt and pepper, and chopped fresh mint or basil, or enjoy as is! Plenty of grated Parmesan cheese is always welcome, too.

Leftover Roasted Carrots →
Cumin-Spiced Carrot Soup

In a medium pot over medium heat, cook *1 cup of leftover roasted carrots* (such as Cumin-Spiced Carrots, page 229) with 1 tablespoon butter, 1 chopped yellow onion, 2 cloves minced garlic, and ¼ teaspoon of salt. Stir in 1 small peeled and chopped sweet potato, 1 teaspoon cumin, ½ teaspoon turmeric, and enough stock or water to cover the vegetables by about 1 inch. Bring everything to a boil over high heat. Reduce the heat to medium-low and simmer until the sweet potato is fork-tender, about 30 minutes. Puree the soup until smooth and creamy. Stir in 1 tablespoon lime juice. Season with more salt to taste.

Leftover Roasted Fish →
Brioche Fish Salad Sandwiches

Using a fork, mash about 1 cup of leftover roasted fish (such as Skillet Cilantro-Lime Salmon, page 179) with 2 tablespoons plain Greek yogurt, 1 tablespoon lemon juice, 1 teaspoon Dijon mustard, 2 tablespoons chopped fresh parsley, ¼ cup diced celery, ¼ cup diced cucumber, and ¼ teaspoon each of salt and pepper. Pile the fish salad into a brioche bun, top with a crisp Bibb lettuce leaf, and enjoy.

Leftover Roasted or Grilled Chicken →
Mediterranean-Style Roasted Chicken Salad

Using two forks, shred leftover roasted or grilled chicken (such as Cast-Iron Sumac Chicken, page 209) into bite-size pieces to make about 1 cup total. Add the shredded chicken to a small bowl with 2 tablespoons Greek yogurt, 1 teaspoon pomegranate molasses, the zest and juice of 1 lemon, 2 tablespoons sliced almonds, 1 tablespoon raisins, and 1 tablespoon chopped fresh dill. Toss this roasted chicken salad with dressed greens or pile it between soft sandwich bread.

Leftover Tomato Soup →
Zaatar Baked Ziti with Peas

Add 4 cups of leftover tomato soup (such as Roasted Tomato Soup with Labneh, page 140) to a 9 × 13-inch baking dish with 4 cups al dente–cooked rigatoni (from about 12 ounces of dry rigatoni). Stir in 1 bag of frozen peas. Evenly scatter everything with 1½ cups shredded low-moisture mozzarella cheese, 1 cup panko breadcrumbs, and 2 tablespoons zaatar. Bake, uncovered, at 375°F until the cheese is golden brown and bubbly, 25 to 30 minutes. Top with fresh parsley right before serving.

Leftover Broccoli → **Lemony Broccoli & Quinoa Pilaf**

Finely chop 2 cups of leftover cooked broccoli (such as Lemon-Feta Broccoli, page 237) and add to a medium bowl. Add the zest and juice of 1 small lemon and then stir in 2 tablespoons olive oil, 1 tablespoon balsamic vinegar, 1 teaspoon Dijon mustard, and ¼ teaspoon salt until evenly coated. Stir in 2 cups cooked quinoa, ½ cup chopped toasted almonds, and 1 teaspoon seven spice (such as my homemade Seven Spice, page 259). Scatter with chopped fresh mint or parsley before serving.

Leftover Labneh → **Zesty Marinated Chicken Thighs**

Mix ½ cup of leftover labneh (such as my homemade Labneh, page 258), 2 tablespoons olive oil, the zest and juice of 1 lime, 1 tablespoon zaatar, 1 teaspoon onion powder, 1 teaspoon garlic powder, and ½ teaspoon of salt in a large bowl. Add about 1 pound of bone-in, skin-on chicken thighs. Use your hands to spread the marinade evenly over the chicken. Rest at room temperature for 20 minutes, then roast at 400°F on a baking sheet until the chicken is browned and crisp, about 45 minutes.

Leftover Whipped Ricotta & Honey-Glazed Peaches → **Honey-Peach Tart**

Roughly chop 2 cups of leftover stone fruit (such as my Whipped Ricotta & Honey-Glazed Peaches on page 285) and set aside in a small bowl. Roll out 1 sheet of thawed store-bought puff pastry (from one 14-ounce package or half of a 17.3-ounce package). Evenly spread the rolled-out pastry with the peach-ricotta mixture, leaving a 1-inch border around the edges. Brush the exposed edges with an egg wash (1 beaten egg yolk whisked with a splash of milk). Bake at 350°F until the pastry is puffed and browned, about 30 minutes. Drizzle with more honey before slicing and serving.

1

Breakfast

Walnut Date Oatmeal

Serves 4   Active Time: 5 minutes   Total Time: 25 minutes

If you walk into my house on any weekday morning, you'll find my family and me enjoying oats every which way: warm and spiced in the winter, cold with fresh fruit in the summer, tossed into muffins, simmered on the stove, shaken in a jar and stored in the fridge—I could go on. (There's a reason I started an oat-based company, Oath!) And this simple, gently sweet oatmeal is one of my favorite recipes of the bunch. Simmering dates in the same water you'll use to make your oatmeal makes them extra soft and creamy— and it infuses the cooking water with the perfect amount of caramel sweetness. It's a subtle layer of flavor that's so worth a few extra minutes on the stove. It's also pretty flexible; I like Medjool dates and 2% milk, but feel free to use whatever dates and milk you have on hand. And it's easy to reheat—just add a splash of milk or water to loosen things up, since the oatmeal will thicken as it settles.

½ **cup pitted Medjool dates,** chopped

2 cups 2% milk

2 cups rolled oats

½ **teaspoon ground cinnamon**

Salt

½ **cup walnuts,** coarsely chopped

1. In a medium saucepan over high heat, bring 2 cups of water to a boil. Reduce the heat to medium-low and add the dates. Cook, stirring occasionally, until the dates are very soft, about 5 minutes.

2. Add the milk, oats, cinnamon, and a pinch of salt to the saucepan. Continue to cook over medium-low, stirring occasionally, until the oats are tender and creamy, 8 to 10 minutes.

3. Divide the oatmeal into four bowls. Add the walnuts on top and enjoy warm.

My Four Favorite Overnight Oats

Chocolate Pomegranate, Peanut Butter & Jelly, Blueberry Lemon, and Mango Sesame

Serves 1 | Active Time: 5 minutes | Total Time: 5 minutes (plus overnight resting)

These oats are so easy and flexible, it's no wonder they are on constant rotation in my house. I make a few servings at a time to have on hand all week, which is also a great task for kids if you'd like to get them helping in the kitchen. And though the variations on overnight oats are basically endless (it's the most searched recipe on my website!), I tend to return again and again to this simple recipe with four different takes on flavor. (By the way, you could just eat the base recipe alone, without the toppings, if you'd like.) Feel free to use frozen fruit instead of fresh or to enjoy these oats warmed through instead of cold from the fridge. That's actually how my daughter, Carine, prefers them!

Base
½ cup rolled oats
½ cup almond milk
¼ cup Greek yogurt
1 tablespoon chia seeds
1 tablespoon maple syrup

Chocolate Pomegranate
¼ cup chocolate chips
1 tablespoon cocoa powder
1 teaspoon pomegranate molasses
Pinch of salt

Peanut Butter & Jelly
¼ cup diced strawberries
1 tablespoon strawberry jam
1 tablespoon peanut butter
1 tablespoon crushed peanuts

Blueberry Lemon
¼ cup blueberries
Zest of 1 lemon
1 tablespoon shredded coconut
½ teaspoon vanilla extract

Mango Sesame
¼ cup cubed mango
1 tablespoon tahini
1 teaspoon toasted sesame seeds
½ teaspoon ground cinnamon

1. In a small resealable container, bowl, or jar, combine the oats, milk, yogurt, chia seeds, maple syrup, and any of the additional flavor combinations. Stir until everything is combined and the ingredients are well distributed. Tightly seal.

2. Place the oats in the fridge for at least 3 hours or up to overnight to allow the oats to set and soften. When you're ready to eat, enjoy the oats cold or warmed through. Garnish with additional toppings, if you'd like.

Orange-Pistachio French Toast Casserole

Serves 12   Active Time: 20 minutes   Total Time: 1 hour and 15 minutes

I can't think of a better make-ahead brunch than this citrusy, just-sweet-enough baked French toast casserole. Studded with dates, pistachios, and an easy orange-scented custard (made right in the blender), it's the best dish for pleasing a hungry crowd with minimal effort. If you'd like, you can prepare this baked French toast through step three the night before and store it tightly covered in the fridge overnight. Then carry on from step four and bake it in the morning while you enjoy your coffee. This is a great option for entertaining or if you have overnight guests!

Olive oil cooking spray

8 large eggs

1¼ cups almond milk

¾ cup orange juice

1 tablespoon freshly grated orange zest

1 teaspoon vanilla extract

½ teaspoon ground nutmeg

¼ teaspoon salt

1 large loaf of French or Italian bread, cut into ½-inch slices

1½ cups pitted chopped Medjool dates, divided

Maple syrup, for serving

¼ cup finely chopped pistachios, for serving

1. Preheat the oven to 350°F. Grease a 9 × 13-inch baking dish with cooking spray.

2. To a blender, add the eggs, milk, orange juice and zest, vanilla, nutmeg, and salt. Blend on high speed until smooth.

3. Arrange the bread in the prepared baking dish. Scatter most of the dates evenly over the bread and then pour the egg mixture over the bread and dates, making sure the bread is coated well with the custard.

4. Bake the casserole until a toothpick inserted in the middle comes out clean with a few moist crumbs attached, 40 to 45 minutes.

5. Drizzle the casserole with the maple syrup right when it comes out of the oven and sprinkle the remaining dates and pistachios on top. Allow the casserole to cool for at least 10 minutes before slicing and serving.

Zaatar Manakeesh

Makes 12 flatbreads | Active Time: 30 minutes | Total Time: 2 hours and 30 minutes

Manakeesh are Mediterranean flatbreads that are often eaten for breakfast. You may have seen these flatbreads in Lebanese restaurants, bakeries, or, if you're really lucky, in someone's home kitchen—the smell of freshly baked manakeesh is truly special! There is a wide variety of possible toppings, but I gravitate toward aromatic zaatar mixed with olive oil. I love slathering them with Labneh (page 258) for breakfast with a cup of Arabic tea.

1 cup warm water

1 packet (2¼ teaspoons) **instant yeast**

3 cups all-purpose flour, plus more for dusting

1 teaspoon salt

¾ cup olive oil, divided

⅔ cup zaatar

Labneh, for serving (optional; page 258)

1. In a large bowl or the bowl of a stand mixer fitted with the hook attachment, mix the water, yeast, flour, and salt until it comes together into a shaggy mixture. Add ¼ cup of the oil and, using your hands in the bowl or the dough hook, knead the dough until it transforms into a smooth, springy ball, 5 to 7 minutes.

2. Cover the bowl with a slightly damp clean kitchen towel. Set the bowl aside at room temperature until the dough has risen to double its volume, 60 to 90 minutes.

3. Preheat the oven to 450°F. Line a large baking sheet with parchment paper.

4. Divide the dough into 12 pieces and shape them into balls; set aside on the baking sheet and cover with a slightly damp clean kitchen towel. Let the dough balls rest for 10 minutes.

5. Lightly dust a flat surface with flour, then take a ball of dough and roll it into a flat palm-size disk about ¼ inch thick and 4 inches in diameter. Place the flatbread back on the prepared baking sheet; cover again with the towel while you work on the rest. Repeat with the remaining dough. Use a fork to prick a few holes in each flatbread (to prevent air pockets).

6. In a small bowl, mix the zaatar with the remaining ½ cup oil until it forms a spreadable mixture. Spread a scant tablespoon of the mixture evenly over the top of each flatbread.

7. Bake the manakeesh until they are puffed and browned on the bottom, 10 to 15 minutes. Enjoy with the labneh (if using).

Strawberry Rose Pancakes

Makes about 8 (6-inch) pancakes　｜　Active Time: 20 minutes　｜　Total Time: 20 minutes

Pancakes for me looked a little different growing up. Inspired by atayef—airy, slightly sweet Mediterranean pancakes—they were stuffed, fried, and soaked in a floral-scented simple syrup. To play off that flavor for an easier weekend breakfast or brunch, I created these pancakes as a modern riff on a traditional Lebanese recipe. Bursting with fresh strawberries and a hint of rose, these pancakes are kind of sophisticated and deceptively simple. They're perfect with just a drizzle of maple syrup, but you could also serve them with some whipped Greek yogurt and honey.

1 cup milk

1 large egg

2 tablespoons (¼ stick) **unsalted butter,** melted, plus more for cooking

1 teaspoon rose water

1 cup all-purpose flour

1 tablespoon sugar

2 teaspoons baking powder

¼ teaspoon salt

1 cup strawberries, hulled and finely chopped, plus more for serving

Maple syrup, for serving

1. In a large bowl, whisk the milk, egg, butter, and rose water until smooth. Gently stir in the flour, sugar, baking powder, and salt until everything is combined (a few lumps are okay). Stir in the strawberries.

2. Coat a griddle or large nonstick skillet with butter over medium heat. Pour the batter onto the griddle or into the pan ⅓ cup at a time, forming pancakes that are about 6 inches in diameter and making sure there is a little space between each pancake. Cook the pancakes on one side until small bubbles start to form on the top and the edges begin to brown, 2 to 3 minutes. Flip each pancake; cook on the second side until golden brown, 1 to 2 minutes longer. Serve immediately with the maple syrup.

My Four Favorite Avocado Toasts

Honey Pistachio, Zaatar Tomato, Strawberry Basil, and Feta Mint

Makes 4 toasts | Active Time: 5 minutes | Total Time: 5 minutes

Does the world need another recipe for avocado toast? Probably not. But avocado toast is so versatile, and I'm obsessed with all the ways you can top it. While I often fall back on rich, creamy avocado smashed over hearty bread and topped with fried eggs, I'll just as often skip the eggs and opt for these Mediterranean-inspired toppings. Each toast is bursting with bright, delicious flavors that will take your avocado-toast game to the next level! And if you're skeptical of any of these combinations, just know that my kids were as well. "Strawberries with avocado?" My son, Adam, looked at me suspiciously. But they agreed: these toasts taste just as good as they look.

Base

1 ripe avocado

1 teaspoon lemon juice

Salt and black pepper

4 slices whole-grain bread, toasted

Topping Combinations

Sliced cherry tomatoes, zaatar, and olive oil

Crumbled feta cheese, chopped fresh mint, and olive oil

Sliced strawberries, chopped fresh basil, and ground sumac

Chopped pistachios, lemon zest, and honey

1. In a small bowl, combine the avocado, lemon juice, and salt and pepper to taste, and use a fork to mash everything together.

2. Divide the mashed avocado between the 4 slices of bread. Add your desired topping combination and serve immediately.

Sesame Banana Bread

Makes 1 (9-inch) loaf | Active Time: 20 minutes | Total Time: 1 hour and 5 minutes

The sweet banana in this bread really highlights the nutty tahini and toasted sesame seeds. It has the ideal level of sweetness and heartiness to complement a cup of coffee, but it's not out of place with a scoop of ice cream for dessert. My mom bakes a few desserts where she uses tahini to grease the bottom of a parchment-lined pan instead of using oil or butter. I love adopting this trick for Mediterranean-inspired baked goods like this one because it adds more sesame flavor throughout. And if you ever find yourself with a few lingering slices of this banana bread (a rare occurrence in my house), it's also ideal for toasting—the outside edges get all browned and delicious while the inside stays moist and soft. A bit of salted butter really takes it to the next level.

½ **cup tahini,** plus more for greasing the pan

1¾ **cups all-purpose flour**

¼ **cup plus 2 tablespoons sesame seeds,** divided

2 **teaspoons ground cinnamon**

1 **teaspoon baking soda**

¼ **teaspoon salt**

¼ **cup** (½ stick) **unsalted butter,** softened

¼ **cup granulated sugar**

¼ **cup** (packed) **dark brown sugar**

2 **large eggs**

3 **ripe bananas,** mashed

1 **teaspoon vanilla extract**

1. Preheat the oven to 350°F. Line a 9 × 5-inch loaf pan with parchment paper so there are at least 2 inches of overhanging parchment on each side. Using a pastry brush, evenly grease the sides and bottom of the parchment with tahini.

2. In a medium bowl, whisk the flour, ¼ cup of the sesame seeds, the cinnamon, baking soda, and salt. Set aside.

3. In a large bowl using an electric hand mixer, cream the tahini, butter, granulated sugar, and brown sugar together on medium-high speed until the mixture is fluffy and about double its original volume, 2 minutes. Whisk in the eggs one at a time, then whisk in the bananas and vanilla. Using a rubber spatula, gently fold in the dry ingredients until no streaks of flour remain.

4. Pour the batter into the prepared pan and evenly smooth the surface. Sprinkle the remaining 2 tablespoons sesame seeds over the top. Bake the banana bread until a toothpick inserted in the center of the loaf comes out clean, 50 to 55 minutes. Cool the banana bread in the pan on a cooling rack completely before slicing and serving.

Spiced Olive Oil Oat Muffins

Makes 12 muffins | Active Time: 15 minutes | Total Time: 50 minutes

These muffins might be the quiet champion of the breakfast world. They freeze well, they come together in one bowl and one muffin tin, and they're packed with rolled oats, tangy Greek yogurt, rich olive oil, and warming spices like cinnamon and cardamom. They're inviting and super delicious when eaten warm from the oven, but they're also somehow just as good (if not even a little better?!) the next day. These muffins provide a nice base if you'd like to add a half cup of grated apple, raisins, and/or toasted nuts and seeds to the batter, but I usually prefer them as you see them here.

1½ cups plus 2 tablespoons rolled oats, divided

¾ cup plus 2 tablespoons (packed) **light brown sugar,** divided

1½ cups all-purpose flour

2 teaspoons ground cinnamon

1 teaspoon ground cardamom

1½ teaspoons baking powder

½ teaspoon baking soda

¼ teaspoon salt

2 large eggs

1¾ cups whole-milk Greek yogurt

¾ cup olive oil

1 teaspoon vanilla extract

1. Preheat the oven to 350°F. Line a 12-cup muffin pan with paper liners.

2. In a small bowl, mix 2 tablespoons of the oats with 2 tablespoons of the sugar and set aside.

3. In a large bowl, whisk the remaining 1½ cups oats and ¾ cup sugar with the flour, cinnamon, cardamom, baking powder, baking soda, and salt. Make a well in the center of the bowl. In the middle of the well, whisk the eggs, yogurt, oil, and vanilla. Gently stir the dry ingredients into the wet ingredients until no streaks of flour remain.

4. Using an ice cream scoop, portion the batter into the prepared muffin pan, filling each cup all the way to the top. Scatter the top of each muffin with the reserved oat-sugar mixture. Bake the muffins until they're firm yet springy to the touch and a toothpick inserted in the center comes out clean, 30 to 35 minutes. Let the muffins cool in the pan before serving.

Scrambled Eggs & Labneh Pita

Serves 2 | Active Time: 10 minutes | Total Time: 10 minutes

In the Middle East, it's more common to have savory breakfasts than sweet ones. For a quick breakfast when I was growing up, my mom would make us scrambled eggs rolled in Arabic-style pita, a wider, flatter kind of pita bread you can find at most Middle Eastern markets. She would spread labneh over the edges of the pita before rolling it up, which kept the scrambled eggs from falling out—so practical and delicious! I now make this for my kids and take it up a notch with some zaatar, olive oil, and fresh mint leaves. Sometimes I'll also add basil, sliced cucumbers, and ripe tomatoes. If you can't find Arabic-style pita around you, feel free to swap in the smaller, puffier pita breads often found at the supermarket and fold them more like a taco than a burrito. It will still be delicious.

4 large eggs

¼ teaspoon salt

1 tablespoon olive oil, plus more for drizzling

Black pepper

2 Arabic-style pita breads

4 tablespoons Labneh (page 258)

1 tablespoon zaatar

¼ cup torn fresh mint

1. In a small bowl, beat the eggs with 1 tablespoon of water and the salt.

2. Heat the oil in a small nonstick skillet over medium heat. Pour in the eggs. Let the eggs cook undisturbed until the outside edges begin to set, about 30 seconds. Using a heat-proof spatula, gently and repeatedly stir the eggs until they're cooked through and have lost any wetness, 2 to 3 minutes. Season with pepper.

3. Place the pitas on a flat surface. Divide the labneh and zaatar evenly between the center of both pitas and drizzle a little oil on top. Use the back of a spoon to spread the labneh-zaatar mixture from the center of the pita outward, leaving about an inch around the edge. Divide the scrambled eggs between the 2 pitas and top with the mint. Roll and enjoy!

Cheesy Squash Omelet

Serves 1 | Active Time: 10 minutes | Total Time: 25 minutes

I'm not sure why, but Mexican squash is very popular in Arabic recipes. We call it kousa, and it's the most common type of squash we use—we'll stuff it with rice and spiced beef, simmer it in soups, toss it into stir-fries, and cook it into fluffy, cheesy omelets. And if you can't find Mexican squash in your local grocery store, zucchini is a perfect substitute. This is my mom's favorite way to make eggs, and the smell of these vegetables cooking in warm olive oil always reminds me of her. She usually skips the cheese, but I say, what's an omelet without cheese?

2 large eggs

1 tablespoon olive oil

¼ cup finely chopped red onion

¼ cup finely chopped seeded red bell pepper

1 small Mexican squash or zucchini, finely chopped

¼ teaspoon salt

1 garlic clove, minced

2 tablespoons shredded low-moisture mozzarella cheese

1. In a small bowl, beat the eggs with 1 tablespoon of water. Set aside.

2. Heat the oil in a small nonstick skillet over medium heat. Add the onion, pepper, squash, and salt. Cook until the vegetables are tender, 7 to 9 minutes. Add the garlic and continue cooking, stirring constantly, until very fragrant, about 30 seconds.

3. Spread the vegetables evenly in the skillet. Pour in the eggs, swirling the skillet so the eggs evenly distribute around the bottom. Let the eggs cook undisturbed until the outside edges begin to set, about 30 seconds. Using a heat-proof spatula, gently push the cooked eggs from the edge of the skillet toward the center, tilting and rotating the skillet to allow any wet egg to flow into the empty spaces. When the eggs look mostly set with a few wet patches, add the mozzarella.

4. Gently wiggle the spatula under one side of the eggs and fold it over the other side to create a half-moon shape. Reduce the heat to the lowest setting possible. Continue to cook the folded omelet until the cheese is melty, about 1 minute longer. Enjoy immediately.

Shakshuka with Feta

Serves 4 | Active Time: 25 minutes | Total Time: 45 minutes

Shakshuka is a well-loved Mediterranean and North African breakfast staple. The smell of poached eggs in a spiced tomato sauce filled with onions and bell peppers always puts me at ease. I love dipping a piece of crusty bread or pita in that amazing sauce, which is remarkably simple for all of its flavor. Best of all, most of these ingredients are probably already in your pantry. This is one of those perfect back-pocket recipes that's totally doable for dinner and great for impromptu visitors—you can always sneak an extra egg or two into the sauce.

1 tablespoon olive oil

1 yellow onion, halved and thinly sliced

1 red bell pepper, halved, seeded, and thinly sliced

2 garlic cloves, minced

1 teaspoon ground cumin

1 teaspoon paprika

1 teaspoon ground sumac

½ teaspoon salt

½ teaspoon black pepper

2 (14.5-ounce) **cans diced tomatoes**

6 large eggs

¼ cup crumbled feta cheese, for serving

¼ cup chopped fresh cilantro, for serving

Crusty bread, for serving

1. Heat the oil in a large skillet over medium heat, then add the onion and bell pepper. Cook until the vegetables are soft, 10 to 12 minutes. Add the garlic, cumin, paprika, sumac, salt, and black pepper. Cook, stirring constantly, until fragrant, about 30 seconds longer.

2. Pour the tomatoes into the skillet. Bring the mixture to a boil over medium-high heat, stirring frequently and scraping up any browned bits from the bottom of the pan. Reduce the heat to medium-low. Simmer until thickened and stew-like, 10 to 15 minutes longer.

3. Using a wooden spoon, create six small wells in the tomato sauce. Gently crack an egg into each well.

4. Cover the pan with a fitted lid. Continue cooking the shakshuka until the egg whites are set and the yolks are cooked to your liking, 5 to 8 minutes.

5. Serve the shakshuka right from the skillet with the feta and cilantro scattered on top. Serve with the crusty bread for dipping.

Pesto Baked Eggs

Serves 4 | Active Time: 5 minutes | Total Time: 20 minutes

Did you see those pesto eggs that took the Internet by storm a while ago? It seemed like everyone's home kitchen contained an egg and some pesto frying in a skillet. The idea inspired me to create a hands-off approach so I could pop a few in the oven on a weekend morning while getting ready for the day. Between the velvety yolks and the savory green pesto, these baked eggs became my go-to way to feed a group of people without much active effort. (This is also one of my ideal solo dinners—I just divide the recipe by four.) Enjoyed with a piece of crusty bread for soaking up those pesto-y yolks, this is one of those feel-good meals that always hits the spot.

8 tablespoons pesto

8 large eggs

¼ teaspoon salt

¼ teaspoon black pepper

Crusty bread, for serving

1. Preheat the oven to 375°F.

2. Evenly brush four ovenproof 4-ounce ramekins with the pesto and crack 2 eggs into each. Sprinkle the salt and pepper on top. Place the ramekins on a large baking sheet.

3. Transfer the baking sheet with the filled ramekins into the oven. Bake the eggs until the whites are just set, 17 to 21 minutes. Serve with the crusty bread for dipping.

My Three Favorite Smoothies

Mint Chocolate, Sweet Greens, and Triple Berry Yogurt

Serves 2 | Active Time: 5 minutes | Total Time: 5 minutes

I've come to realize that I really want all my smoothies to taste like milkshakes. Seriously, flavor is so important when it comes to the food that makes us feel good! These smoothies are filled with fruits and vegetables, but they don't skimp on the delicious flavors that make me savor every sip. The Mint Chocolate Smoothie tastes rich and luxurious—I also love adding a half cup of cold brew or leftover coffee if I'm looking for an extra energy boost. Sweet Greens is for those mornings I'm craving something lively and bright green to give my day a produce-heavy jump-start. And the Triple Berry Yogurt Smoothie is such a crowd-pleaser—it's nourishing, filling, and the color of strawberry ice cream. It also gives me the opportunity to ask people, "Did you know pomegranates are botanically in the berry family?"

Mint Chocolate

2 frozen bananas

2 pitted Medjool dates

2 tablespoons almond butter

1 tablespoon cocoa powder

¼ cup (packed) **fresh mint leaves**

1½ cups almond milk
(or any milk you like)

Sweet Greens

2 frozen bananas

½ cup frozen cubed pineapple

1 cup (packed) **baby spinach**

2 kale leaves, stemmed

2 Persian cucumbers

1½ cups coconut water

Triple Berry Yogurt

1 frozen banana

1 cup frozen strawberries

1 cup frozen raspberries

¼ cup Greek yogurt

¼ cup rolled oats

1 teaspoon pomegranate molasses

1½ cups milk (or your favorite plant-based milk)

In a blender, add the ingredients of your chosen flavor combination and blend on high speed until smooth and creamy, 30 seconds to 1 minute. Pour into two glasses and enjoy immediately.

2

Appetizers

My Four Favorite Stuffed Dates

Labneh Pistachio, Goat Cheese Sumac, Mozzarella Basil, and Feta Mint

Makes 16 stuffed dates | Active Time: 15 minutes | Total Time: 15 minutes

Dates are integral to Mediterranean culture. For me, they also play a huge role during the Islamic month of Ramadan when I fast from dawn to sunset for thirty days and break my daily fast with one date. It's well known in Muslim tradition that dates are the perfect food for breaking a fast since their high sugar and fiber content instantly fuels an empty stomach and restores blood sugar levels. For me, I've taken this sentiment as a signal to incorporate nourishing, energy-boosting dates into my daily diet. I snack on them frequently with nuts between meals to satisfy my hunger, and I love serving them as an appetizer with different types of cheeses and pops of flavor to show off their sweet and savory potential. Each combination here makes four dates, so you'll end up with sixteen dates total with four different flavors. But if you prefer to make all the dates with one kind of filling, like Feta Mint, just quadruple the given amounts!

16 large Medjool dates

Labneh Pistachio

1 tablespoon Labneh (page 258)

1 tablespoon honey

16 pistachios, shelled

Goat Cheese Sumac

1 tablespoon goat cheese

4 whole walnuts

¼ teaspoon ground sumac

Mozzarella Basil

4 small slices fresh mozzarella

4 sun-dried tomatoes, thinly sliced

1 large basil leaf, sliced

Feta Mint

1 tablespoon crumbled feta cheese

2 teaspoons freshly grated lemon zest

4 fresh mint leaves

1. Use a paring knife to slit the dates lengthwise. Remove and discard the pits.

2. Use a spoon or your hands to evenly fill each date with the fillings, until you have 16 dates total with 4 different fillings.

Baba's Classic Hummus

Serves 6 | Active Time: 25 minutes | Total Time: 25 minutes

My dad, Baba, makes the best hummus. Like all traditional Lebanese hummus recipes, his version only has five ingredients (plus his secret ingredient of a few ice cubes, which creates the creamiest texture!). Yet he has somehow created the best balance between each one, making me want to eat it straight out of the food processor every time. And here's the thing: my dad doesn't measure anything. He just throws the ingredients into the food processor, eyeballing each amount and stopping the machine a minimum of five times to taste and adjust. Each lemon has a different level of acidity; each garlic clove has a unique pungency; every brand of canned chickpeas has a distinct texture. After many years of enjoying his classic hummus, I've realized that Baba's recipe can never be truly measured or replicated—but this is as close to it as I can get. I even asked him to give me his okay on this recipe, and Baba gives it two thumbs up!

1 (15-ounce) **can chickpeas**

3 tablespoons lemon juice, plus more as needed

2 tablespoons tahini

2 garlic cloves

¾ teaspoon salt, plus more as needed

3 ice cubes

Extra-virgin olive oil, for serving

Paprika, for serving

Chopped fresh parsley, for serving

1. Place the chickpeas in a large bowl of warm water. Rub them with your fingers to release the skins, which will easily float to the surface of the water. Skim the skins from the water with a slotted spoon and discard. (This is an optional step, but peeling the chickpeas is what yields a super creamy texture.) Drain and dry the chickpeas as thoroughly as possible.

2. Transfer the chickpeas to a food processor and pulse into a fine, breadcrumb-like texture, scraping down the sides as needed, about 15 seconds total.

3. Add the lemon juice, tahini, garlic, salt, and ice cubes. Blend until completely smooth, about 5 minutes.

4. Spread the hummus onto a plate or into a bowl, sweeping the hummus with the back of a spoon to create swirls for catching the oil. Drizzle the hummus with the oil and then sprinkle it with the paprika and parsley before serving.

Not My Baba's Ghanoush

Serves 6 | Active Time: 15 minutes | Total Time: 1 hour 15 minutes

Okay, Baba also makes the best baba ghanoush—a classic Mediterranean dip made of silky roasted and pureed eggplant. What can I say, the man is good with the dips! And yet this recipe is not his baba ghanoush because my dad firmly believes in roasting the eggplant on an open flame or on the grill. To me, an accident-prone home cook, roasting eggplant on an open flame makes me a little anxious, and grilling outside is only practical about four months out of the year in Michigan. So instead I opt to roast the eggplant in the oven, a method that's more hands-off and guaranteed not to burn any fingers. Trust me, you'll still love the roasted, caramelized flavor balanced with that pop of garlic and fresh lemon juice.

1 large eggplant

¼ cup tahini

3 tablespoons lemon juice

2 garlic cloves, peeled

1 teaspoon salt

Extra-virgin olive oil, for serving

Pomegranate seeds, for serving

Pita, for serving

1. Preheat the oven to 400°F.

2. Prick the eggplant all over with a fork and then wrap it tightly in aluminum foil. Roast for 45 to 55 minutes, until the eggplant is completely fork-tender. Allow the eggplant to cool, unwrapped, for at least 15 minutes.

3. When the eggplant has cooled enough so you can handle it, cut off the top and peel off the skin, discarding it. Place the peeled eggplant in a food processor or blender. Add the tahini, lemon juice, garlic, and salt. Pulse until smooth but still somewhat chunky, about 1 minute.

4. Transfer the baba ghanoush into a serving bowl. Top with the oil and a scattering of pomegranate seeds. Enjoy with pita.

Toasted Zaatar Pita Chips with Muhammara

Serves 6 | Active Time: 20 minutes | Total Time: 20 minutes

I think I ate more pita chips growing up than potato chips—seriously! That's because my mom would fry up a few Arabic pita breads each week to add to Mama's Fattoush Salad (page 101), and we would snack on the rest of the chips with Labneh (page 258) throughout the week. Instead of deep frying the pita chips like she used to, my mom now bakes them in the oven. The flavor is so much lighter this way, and the cleanup is definitely easier. It's also my trick for using up stale-ish Arabic pita that's no longer soft and pliable. (And my kids love them!) Lately I have been serving these zaatar-spiced chips alongside bright, sweet, and smoky muhammara, a dip that originates from Syria but is also super popular in Lebanon. It's one of my all-time favorites and a cinch to make at home.

Pita Chips

2 Arabic-style pita breads, cut into small chip-size triangles

3 tablespoons olive oil

1 tablespoon zaatar

Muhammara

1 (12-ounce) **jar roasted red peppers,** drained

1 cup walnuts, toasted

½ cup breadcrumbs

3 tablespoons olive oil, plus more for serving

1 tablespoon pomegranate molasses

1 garlic clove

1 teaspoon ground cumin

¼ teaspoon ground cayenne pepper

¼ teaspoon salt

1. Preheat the oven to 425°F. Line a baking sheet with parchment paper.

2. Add the pita triangles, oil, and zaatar on the prepared baking sheet. Toss everything with your hands to combine and spread the pita in a single layer. Toast, flipping once halfway through, until the chips are browned and crisp, 7 to 10 minutes. The pita chips will continue to crisp as they cool.

3. Meanwhile, to a food processor, add the red peppers, walnuts, breadcrumbs, oil, pomegranate molasses, garlic, cumin, cayenne, and salt; pulse until smooth and spreadable. Spoon the muhammara into a serving bowl and top with a drizzle of oil. Serve alongside the pita chips.

Zaatar Focaccia

Makes 12 slices | Active Time: 10 minutes | Total Time: 2 hours 10 minutes

I used to think focaccia was an intimidating recipe, but it's really quite simple: you just mix a few staple ingredients together and give everything time to rise. The one-hour rising time in this recipe is perfect for very busy (or hungry) days, but you can also let the dough proof at room temperature for up to twelve hours to lend the focaccia a slightly springier crumb and heartier flavor. Before baking—and this is the best part— you create dimples in the dough by pressing it into the pan with your fingertips. It's a pretty satisfying process, and the end result always looks so fancy for such a delicious, fuss-free homemade bread. The zaatar takes this focaccia to a whole new level—a zesty Mediterranean one that calls for plenty of labneh for dipping!

7 tablespoons olive oil, divided

3½ cups all-purpose flour

1½ cups warm water

1 tablespoon instant yeast

½ teaspoon salt

3 tablespoons zaatar

Labneh, for serving (optional; page 258)

1. In a large bowl, combine 3 tablespoons of the oil with the flour, water, yeast, salt, and zaatar. Using a rubber spatula, stir all of the ingredients together until combined, scraping down the sides of the bowl as needed.

2. Using your hands, gently shape and knead the dough together until it forms a neat ball. (You don't need to really knead, you're just bringing the dough together.) Cover the bowl with a clean, slightly damp kitchen towel. Set the bowl aside at room temperature until the dough has risen to double its volume, at least 1 hour and up to 12 hours.

3. Coat a 9 × 9-inch baking dish with 1 tablespoon of the oil. Transfer the dough to the prepared pan and, using your fingers, spread it over the surface of the pan until it reaches each edge. Cover the dough once again and rest at room temperature for 30 minutes longer.

4. Meanwhile, preheat the oven to 400°F.

5. Drizzle the dough with the remaining 3 tablespoons of oil. Using your fingers, gently press dimples all over the surface of the dough.

6. Bake the focaccia until it's golden brown and fragrant, 30 to 35 minutes. Remove the focaccia from the oven and allow it to cool in the pan for 10 minutes. Slice into 12 squares and serve with the labneh (if using).

Roasted Garlic Sumac Bread

Serves 8 | Active Time: 10 minutes | Total Time: 1 hour 30 minutes

Have you ever roasted a full head of garlic and noticed how creamy and rich the golden-brown cloves become? Soft, silky roasted garlic is spreadable like butter but infused with the most incredible caramelized, sweet-savory flavor. So, why not swap butter for roasted garlic and create the ultimate garlic bread? And because I love when the dominant flavor in garlic bread is, well, garlic, I use four heads here instead of the standard one or two. I promise it won't be overpowering—it's sneakily mind-blowing and all around pretty fantastic.

4 heads garlic

¼ cup plus 4 teaspoons olive oil, divided

2 tablespoons chopped fresh parsley

1 teaspoon ground sumac

½ teaspoon salt

1 loaf of Italian bread, sliced in half lengthwise

1. Preheat the oven to 400°F. Make four squares of aluminum foil large enough to wrap each head of garlic.

2. Cut the tops from each garlic head to expose the cloves, then place the heads cut side up on the prepared foil. Drizzle each head with 1 teaspoon of the oil, then wrap each one tightly in the foil. Transfer the packets to a baking sheet.

3. Roast the garlic until the cloves are golden brown and completely soft, 50 to 60 minutes (depending on the size of your garlic). Unwrap the foil and let the garlic cool for at least 15 minutes. Set aside the baking sheet and leave the oven on.

4. Using your hands or tongs, squeeze the soft cloves from each head of garlic into a small bowl. Add the remaining ¼ cup oil, the parsley, sumac, and salt; stir to combine.

5. Spread the roasted garlic mixture evenly over the bread halves. Place the garlic bread on the reserved baking sheet and bake until crisp-edged and golden, about 15 minutes. Slice into 8 large or 16 small pieces.

Olive Tapenade Flatbread

Makes 2 flatbreads   Active Time: 15 minutes   Total Time: 15 minutes

Olives are a crucial part of Mediterranean cooking, and there are so many varieties! At any given time, my fridge usually has at least three different kinds of olives because who knows what type of flavor I'm in the mood for on a given day? Rich, fruity Kalamata? Dense, buttery Cerignola or Castelvetrano? Inky cured black olives? Tiny, herby Niçoise? When I have an abundance of olives and want to make room for the fresh crop my brother is bringing in from Lebanon, I make an olive tapenade. It's so versatile and can work with any olives you have on hand. I give my homemade tapenade a boost with something salty, like capers; something savory, like sun-dried tomatoes; and something fresh, like garlic and herbs.

1 cup pitted mixed olives

¼ cup oil-packed sun-dried tomatoes

2 tablespoons capers

2 garlic cloves

2 tablespoons fresh parsley, plus more for serving

2 tablespoons lemon juice

2 large (4-ounce) **naan breads**

1. In a food processor, combine the olives, tomatoes (and any oil that clings to them), capers, garlic, parsley, and lemon juice. Pulse until roughly chopped.

2. Spread the tapenade evenly over the naan. Sprinkle with more parsley before cutting and serving.

Baked Feta Garlic Confit

Serves 8 | Active Time: 10 minutes | Total Time: 1 hour

In early 2021, I made a recipe called Baked Feta Pasta (page 159), and it went viral—seriously, viral! Grocery stores across the country were running out of feta cheese, and thirty million people tuned in to watch me make the now-very-recognizable dish on Feel Good Foodie. This baked feta pasta enthusiasm inspired me to make many more "baked feta" kinds of dishes, which is luckily among my favorite things to eat because my kitchen is now Baked Feta Central. Think of this feta-garlic dip like baked feta meets garlic confit, a hands-off dish that gets cooked low and slow in a bath of olive oil before getting all mixed up into one dippable, magical mixture. The feta becomes puffed and melty, the garlic collapses into sweet-savory perfection in the olive oil, and the rosemary leaves get sizzled until crispy. Mash it all together while it's still warm and you're left with a pretty addictive baked feta riff.

1 (8-ounce) **block of feta cheese**

1 cup peeled garlic cloves

3 sprigs of fresh rosemary

¼ teaspoon crushed red pepper

½ cup extra-virgin olive oil, plus more as needed

Zaatar Focaccia (page 72) **or crusty bread,** for serving

1. Preheat the oven to 325°F.

2. Place the feta in the middle of an 8 × 4-inch loaf pan. Scatter the garlic, rosemary, and crushed red pepper around the sides.

3. Pour the oil over and around all of the ingredients, making sure all of the garlic cloves are just submerged in the oil. Bake, uncovered, until the garlic is completely soft and the feta is melty, about 50 minutes.

4. Use a fork to remove the rosemary from the pan. Strip the crispy rosemary leaves from the stems into a small bowl and set aside, discarding the stems.

5. Use the fork to mash the garlic and feta together. Sprinkle the dip with the crispy rosemary leaves. Serve warm with the Zaatar Focaccia.

Quinoa-Feta Fritters with Labneh-Dill Dip

Makes about 8 fritters | Active Time: 35 minutes | Total Time: 35 minutes

I really believe that my kids will eat anything in fritter form, so fritters are one of the ways I use up leftover grains, like quinoa (which I'm always optimistic I'll eat more of than I do), leftover produce (like parsley that's about to wilt), and leftover cheese, like feta (which is always on hand in my house). Bind all of those ingredients together with egg and breadcrumbs, and you're ready to transform a few humble ingredients into something crisp, golden, and delicious. With these fritters, the sum is truly greater than the original (leftover) parts. The herby labneh dip served alongside is tart, bright, and creamy, and it's also really good the next day as a salad dressing—because leftovers always have a role in this kitchen!

Fritters

2 large eggs

1 cup cooked quinoa

½ cup crumbled feta cheese

½ cup finely chopped red onion

½ cup chopped fresh parsley

2 garlic cloves, minced

¼ teaspoon salt

½ cup panko breadcrumbs

4 tablespoons avocado oil, divided

Labneh-Dill Dip

1 lemon

½ cup Labneh (page 258)

1 teaspoon dried dill

Salt and black pepper

1. In a large bowl, beat the eggs. Stir in the quinoa, feta, onion, parsley, garlic, and salt. Stir in the breadcrumbs; let sit for 2 minutes so the crumbs can absorb some of the moisture. Using a ⅓ measuring cup, scoop, firmly pack, and shape the mixture into 7 to 8 patties.

2. Heat 2 tablespoons of the oil in a large nonstick skillet over medium-high heat. Add half of the patties and cook until browned and crisp, 3 to 4 minutes per side. Transfer the cooked fritters to a large paper towel–lined plate and tent with foil to keep warm. Repeat with the remaining 2 tablespoons oil and the patties.

3. To make the dip, zest and juice the lemon into a small bowl. Whisk in the labneh, dill, and salt and pepper to taste. Serve with the quinoa fritters.

Crispy Cauliflower with Mint-Avocado Crema

Serves 6 | Active Time: 20 minutes | Total Time: 55 minutes

Cauliflower fritters in Arabic are called mshat, *and there are as many variations as there are home cooks. And while I love a fritter in any form (see Quinoa-Feta Fritters with Labneh-Dill Dip, page 82), I was inspired to go rogue with this cauliflower recipe and build plenty of crunchy goodness into the floret itself. This dish has a subtle hint of Mediterranean flavors such as cumin and fresh mint, and I really love that you can throw it all on a baking sheet to crisp in the oven—no standing over hot oil, here. These are so good warm from the oven with the mint-green, labneh-spiked avocado crema for dipping.*

Crispy Cauliflower

Olive oil cooking spray

1 head cauliflower, cut into florets

2 tablespoons cornstarch

2 large eggs, beaten

¾ cup panko breadcrumbs

½ cup grated Parmesan cheese

1 teaspoon ground cumin

1 teaspoon garlic powder

¼ teaspoon salt

¼ teaspoon black pepper

Mint-Avocado Crema

1 lime

1 small ripe avocado

¼ cup Labneh (page 258)

2 tablespoons chopped fresh mint

Salt and black pepper

1. Preheat the oven to 400°F. Place a cooling rack on top of a rimmed baking sheet and coat with the cooking spray.

2. In a medium bowl, sprinkle the cauliflower florets with the cornstarch; toss until evenly coated. Add the eggs and toss again until evenly coated.

3. In a separate medium bowl, combine the panko, Parmesan, cumin, garlic powder, salt, and pepper. One at a time, dredge each cauliflower floret in the panko mixture before transferring it to the cooling rack. Generously spray the florets with cooking spray.

4. Roast the cauliflower florets, flipping halfway through, until they are tender and golden brown, 30 to 35 minutes.

5. Meanwhile, zest and juice the lime into a small bowl. Mash in the avocado until it's as smooth as possible, then add the labneh, mint, and a pinch of salt and pepper; whisk until smooth. Serve the mint-avocado crema alongside the crispy cauliflower.

Labneh-Stuffed Charred Peppers

Makes about 16 peppers | Active Time: 15 minutes | Total Time: 30 minutes

Do you remember the bell pepper "sandwiches" that were popular on social media a while back? It was basically halved peppers slathered with cream cheese and other toppings and enjoyed raw. I wouldn't call it a sandwich, but I definitely enjoyed them! Here's a Midwestern-meets-Mediterranean twist on that idea using tart labneh instead of sweet cream cheese, plus salty olives, mozzarella cheese, and citrusy sumac. Roast them in the oven until charred and melty for a perfect appetizer or after-school snack.

½ **cup Labneh** (page 258)

⅓ **cup shredded low-moisture mozzarella cheese**

¼ **cup chopped fresh parsley**

¼ **cup chopped pitted Kalamata olives**

1 **teaspoon ground sumac**

1 **pound mini sweet bell peppers,** tops removed and insides seeded

Olive oil cooking spray

Salt

1. Preheat the oven to 450°F. Line a large baking sheet with parchment paper.

2. In a small bowl, mix the labneh, mozzarella, parsley, olives, and sumac until well combined.

3. Scoop about 1 tablespoon of the filling into the cavity of each pepper and place them on the prepared baking sheet. Spray the peppers with the cooking spray and season with a pinch of salt. Roast until the peppers are softened and browned and the cheese is melty, 10 to 15 minutes.

Broccoli & Cheese Bulgur Bites

Makes 20 to 24 bites | Active Time: 20 minutes | Total Time: 40 minutes

Everything seems more approachable when it's bite-size, right? I find that I can get my modern-day family excited about ancient Mediterranean grains like bulgur by mixing the cracked wheat with broccoli, melty cheese, and savory spices like cumin and garlic. I then scoop them into tiny balls and bake them up until golden brown on the outside and cheesy on the inside—what's not to love? These one-bite beauties are great on their own or served with a dish of warm marinara for dipping.

½ **cup fine #1 bulgur wheat**

¼ **teaspoon salt**

¼ **teaspoon black pepper**

½ **cup hot water**

1 cup finely chopped broccoli

2 cups shredded Cheddar cheese

1 large egg

2 teaspoons ground cumin

2 teaspoons garlic powder

Prepared marinara sauce, warmed, for serving (optional)

1. Preheat the oven to 400°F. Line a large baking sheet with parchment paper.

2. In a large bowl, stir together the bulgur, salt, pepper, and water. Rest until the bulgur has absorbed all the liquid, about 10 minutes.

3. Fluff the bulgur with a fork, then stir in the broccoli, cheese, egg, cumin, and garlic powder.

4. Using a medium spring-loaded cookie scoop (about 1½ tablespoons), scoop and firmly pack the bulgur mixture into a small ball and add it to the prepared baking sheet. Repeat with the remaining bulgur mixture, leaving a little space in between each bulgur bite.

5. Bake until the cheese is melty and the edges are golden, 20 to 25 minutes. Serve with the marinara (if using) for dipping.

Halloumi Bruschetta

Serves 8 | Active Time: 20 minutes | Total Time: 20 minutes

If you've never had delicious halloumi cheese before, there are two things you should know. First, it doesn't melt! That makes it perfect for grilling, baking, and frying. Second, it's pretty salty. To help with that, I'll sometimes soak halloumi in cold water for half an hour before patting it dry, cooking it, and serving it, especially if it's for someone who has never had it before. But just as often I'll skip that step and instead serve halloumi with something sweet or fresh—or both—to balance out all of those savory flavors. My family usually enjoys halloumi fried with a side of fresh tomatoes and cucumbers. But lately we've been loving halloumi in the form of this bright, savory bruschetta, which is such an epic combination!

2 Roma tomatoes, finely diced

2 garlic cloves, minced

¼ cup chopped fresh basil

2 tablespoons balsamic vinegar

¼ teaspoon black pepper

4 tablespoons olive oil, divided

1 (8-ounce) **block of halloumi,** drained and sliced crosswise into 8 (½-inch) planks

8 (½-inch-thick) **slices of baguette**

1. In a medium bowl, combine the tomatoes, garlic, basil, vinegar, pepper, and 2 tablespoons of the oil. Set aside at room temperature to marinate.

2. Pat the halloumi slices very dry with a paper towel. Set aside.

3. Heat 1 tablespoon of the oil in a grill pan or a heavy-bottomed skillet over medium heat. Add the baguette slices in a single layer. Cook on one side until crisp and golden brown, about 3 minutes. Flip each slice; cook until the second side is golden brown, 2 to 3 minutes longer. Transfer the toasted baguette to a serving platter. Set aside.

4. Wipe out the grill pan. Heat the remaining 1 tablespoon of oil over medium heat. Add the sliced halloumi in a single layer. Cook, undisturbed, until the bottoms are golden brown, 3 to 5 minutes. Flip the halloumi and cook until the other side is also golden brown, 2 to 4 minutes longer.

5. Transfer the halloumi to the serving platter, topping each baguette slice with 1 piece of cheese. Divide the marinated tomatoes evenly on top of the halloumi and serve immediately.

Caramelized Eggplant with Mint Yogurt

Serves 6 | Active Time: 15 minutes | Total Time: 45 minutes

Eggplant does not have the greatest PR in the vegetable kingdom (can we get cauliflower's representation over here?). I get it! Cooked one way, eggplant can be bland or unappetizing But rest assured, treat eggplant with the level of respect it gets in Mediterranean cooking and you will be repaid tenfold. To really see how luxurious and even velvety eggplant can be, roast it in a hot oven with honey, cumin, and tart-sweet pomegranate molasses until it is collapsed and caramelized. Pile it over herby, garlicky Greek yogurt, scatter everything with a handful of fresh pomegranate seeds, and thank me later. Don't forget the pita for dipping!

Caramelized Eggplant

1 large eggplant, cut into 1-inch cubes

3 tablespoons olive oil

2 tablespoons honey

1 teaspoon ground cumin

¼ teaspoon salt

¼ teaspoon black pepper

1 tablespoon pomegranate molasses

Mint Yogurt

½ cup Greek yogurt

¼ cup chopped fresh mint, plus more for serving

1 garlic clove, minced

¼ teaspoon ground cumin

Salt

For serving

Pomegranate seeds

Pita

1. Preheat the oven to 425°F. Line a large baking sheet with parchment paper.

2. Add the eggplant to the baking sheet. Drizzle it with the oil, honey, cumin, salt, and pepper and then use your hands to toss everything together. Roast, stirring once halfway through, until the eggplant is browned and caramelized, 30 to 35 minutes. Drizzle the caramelized eggplant with the pomegranate molasses as soon as it comes out of the oven; toss to coat.

3. Meanwhile, in a small bowl, whisk the yogurt with the mint, garlic, cumin, and a pinch of salt. Spread the mint yogurt on a serving platter and pile the eggplant on top. Scatter with more mint and the pomegranate seeds. Serve with the pita for dipping.

Marinated Olives

Serves 12 | Active Time: 5 minutes | Total Time: 35 minutes

The best way to perk up olives? Marinating them! It's super easy but a little fancy, and they're the perfect thing to throw together if you have last-minute company. I don't pit the olives because they're never pitted at a Lebanese restaurant—part of the experience, in my opinion, is maneuvering your mouth around to get the pit out. If that worries you, feel free to buy pitted olives or gently remove the pits before marinating. I suggest serving these olives with Labneh (page 258) and pita bread for dunking and dipping, but they're just as delicious alone, alongside some toothpicks for catching the olives.

3 cups mixed olives, drained

2 sprigs of fresh rosemary

2 sprigs of fresh thyme

4 garlic cloves, thinly sliced

Zest of 1 lemon

½ teaspoon crushed red pepper

½ cup extra-virgin olive oil

1. In a small saucepan, stir together the olives, rosemary, thyme, garlic, lemon zest, crushed red pepper, and oil. Set the pan over medium-low heat. When the oil is warm and you begin to see a few bubbles simmering gently on the surface, remove the pan from the heat.

2. Transfer the mixture to a small serving bowl and let marinate for 30 minutes before serving.

3

Salads

Tahini Caesar Salad

Serves 6 | Active Time: 30 minutes | Total Time: 30 minutes

If you're not a fan of anchovies in Caesar salads, you're in luck because I make this Caesar with capers instead. Finely chopped capers add a salty, briny kick that's reminiscent of anchovies but keeps this salad, like all of the salads in this book, totally vegetarian. I also like upping my Caesar game by giving it a Mediterranean influence with creamy tahini instead of egg yolks or mayonnaise. It adds a beautiful silkiness and nutty flavor—and makes this dressing completely vegan. If you want the entire recipe to be vegan, just skip the Parmesan on top when serving.

1 lemon

⅓ cup tahini

1 garlic clove, minced

1 tablespoon capers, drained and finely chopped

1 teaspoon Dijon mustard

Salt and black pepper

2 tablespoons olive oil

½ loaf of French bread, cut into 1-inch cubes (about 2 cups)

2 small heads of romaine lettuce, chopped

2 tablespoons shaved Parmesan cheese

1. Zest and juice the lemon into a large serving bowl. Whisk in the tahini, garlic, capers, and mustard until smooth. Whisk in 2 tablespoons of water to thin out the dressing. Season to taste with the salt and pepper. Set aside.

2. Heat the oil in a large skillet over medium heat. Add the bread and cook, tossing frequently, until golden brown and crisp on all sides, 6 to 10 minutes.

3. Add the lettuce and half of the croutons to the bowl with the dressing and toss to combine. Top the salad with the remaining croutons and the Parmesan.

Mama's Fattoush Salad

Serves 6　　Active Time: 20 minutes　　Total Time: 20 minutes

In Arabic, the word fattoush *is derived from* fatteh, *which literally means "crumbs." This makes perfect sense because this popular Mediterranean salad is basically a hodgepodge of lettuce, seasonal vegetables, and a generous portion of fried or baked pita bread for texture and crunch. There are no rules when it comes to the vegetables you use in fattoush, and I love my mom's approach to it. To her, the lettuce, tomatoes, and cucumbers are essential, the dressing is* key, *and everything else is truly optional. When it comes to the pita chips, you can panfry them (like I do in this recipe), deep fry them, bake them, use your favorite store-bought brand, or just skip them all together—it's what my mom does. And when has she ever made anything but delicious fattoush? (Never!)*

Dressing

2 tablespoons lemon juice

1 teaspoon pomegranate molasses

1 teaspoon ground sumac

½ teaspoon dried mint

¼ teaspoon salt

¼ teaspoon black pepper

3 tablespoons extra-virgin olive oil

Fried Pita Bread

3 tablespoons olive oil

1 large Arabic-style pita, cut into small triangles

¼ teaspoon salt

¼ teaspoon black pepper

Salad

1 large head of romaine lettuce, chopped

2 Roma tomatoes, chopped

5 radishes, chopped

2 Persian cucumbers, chopped

½ large green bell pepper, seeded and chopped

2 green onions (whites and greens), sliced

¼ cup chopped fresh parsley

1. In a small bowl, whisk the lemon juice, pomegranate molasses, sumac, mint, salt, and pepper. Slowly stream in the oil, whisking continuously until emulsified. Set aside.

2. Heat the oil in a large skillet over medium heat. Add the pita and season with the salt and pepper. Cook, stirring frequently, until the pita is crisp and golden brown, 5 to 8 minutes. Set aside.

3. In a large serving bowl, add the lettuce, tomatoes, radishes, cucumbers, bell pepper, green onions, and parsley. Pour the dressing over the top and toss to coat. Add the fried pita chips on top of the salad just before serving.

Tabbouleh Salad

Serves 6   Active Time: 20 minutes   Total Time: 20 minutes

Following fattoush, tabbouleh is probably the second-most-popular Lebanese salad. And while this dish has become more well known in the United States, the key difference between traditional tabbouleh and a more Americanized version is the ratio of bulgur to parsley. We don't use parsley as a garnish here—we use it as the main ingredient with the bulgur playing a supporting role. In fact, in an entire large serving bowl of this salad I only use a quarter cup of the cracked whole wheat. Two other good tips for preparing great tabbouleh: make sure to wash and dry the parsley thoroughly (preferably the day before you want to assemble this salad) and use fine #1 bulgur. This kind of bulgur just needs soaking, not cooking. My mother-in-law once shared the brilliant idea of soaking fine bulgur in lemon juice and olive oil instead of water, which really infuses the grain with flavor and makes this tabbouleh extra special.

⅓ **cup extra-virgin olive oil**

3 tablespoons lemon juice

¼ **cup fine #1 bulgur**

3 cups chopped fresh parsley (from about 2 bunches)

2 firm Roma tomatoes, finely chopped

2 green onions (whites and greens), finely chopped

¼ **cup fresh mint leaves,** chopped

¼ **teaspoon salt**

¼ **teaspoon black pepper**

1. In a large bowl, whisk the oil and lemon juice until well combined. Stir in the bulgur. Let the grains soak up the dressing until they are plump and most of the moisture is absorbed, 20 to 30 minutes.

2. Meanwhile, without mixing, add the parsley, tomatoes, green onions, and mint to one side of the bowl with the bulgur.

3. When the bulgur is plump and the lemon–olive oil mixture is mostly absorbed, season with the salt and pepper, and stir everything together until well combined. Serve chilled or at room temperature.

Roasted Chickpea Salad with Labneh Dressing

Serves 4 | Active Time: 15 minutes | Total Time: 45 minutes

It's nice when an ingredient can really show off its strengths in a recipe, and chickpeas definitely play the hero in this salad. They have protein to help give you energy, fiber to help keep you full, and the greatest crunch to help you stay satisfied. This salad works great with a creamy labneh dressing to balance all the savory, hearty flavors in the roasted chickpeas and fresh vegetables. By the way, these crispy chickpeas are also fantastic on their own as a snack or appetizer.

Roasted Chickpeas

1 (15-ounce) **can chickpeas,** rinsed, drained, and dried

1 tablespoon extra-virgin olive oil

¾ teaspoon Seven Spice (page 259 or store-bought)

¼ teaspoon salt

¼ teaspoon black pepper

Dressing

¼ cup Labneh (page 258)

2 tablespoons extra-virgin olive oil

Juice of ½ lemon

1 tablespoon chopped fresh mint

¼ teaspoon salt

¼ teaspoon black pepper

Salad

2 heads romaine lettuce, chopped

3 Persian cucumbers, sliced

1 cup grape tomatoes, halved

½ cup pitted Kalamata olives, roughly chopped

¼ red onion, thinly sliced

1. Preheat the oven to 425°F. Line a small baking sheet with parchment paper.

2. Add the chickpeas to the baking sheet and toss with the oil, seven spice, salt, and pepper until everything is well coated. Spread the chickpeas in a single layer and bake, stirring once halfway through, until they're browned and crispy, 30 to 35 minutes. Let the chickpeas cool for at least 10 minutes—they will continue to crisp as they rest.

3. Meanwhile, in a small bowl, whisk the labneh, oil, lemon juice, mint, salt, and pepper. Set aside.

4. In a large serving bowl, add the lettuce, cucumbers, tomatoes, olives, and onion. Toss with the labneh dressing until evenly coated and top with the roasted chickpeas.

Grilled Halloumi Peach Salad

Serves 6 | Active Time: 15 minutes | Total Time: 25 minutes

Halloumi is one of those magical, non-melting cheeses that tastes like a grilled cheese without the bread when it's seared on a grill or in a hot skillet. I love eating it fresh, too, but it's seriously next level when crisped to golden-brown perfection. Grilled halloumi is tender yet sturdy and deliciously savory, with a robust flavor that adds a fun flair to salads. And because this cheese is rather meaty, it's great for adding to vegetarian salads to make them heartier and more filling. Alongside ripe peaches, walnuts, and a pomegranate molasses–spiked dressing, this salad highlights just how good halloumi can be.

Salad

1 (8-ounce) **block of halloumi,** drained and sliced crosswise into ¼-inch planks

1 tablespoon extra-virgin olive oil

5 ounces spring mix lettuce (about 10 cups)

2 peaches, sliced

¼ cup thinly sliced red onion

⅔ cup walnuts, roughly chopped

Dressing

¼ cup extra-virgin olive oil

3 tablespoons red wine vinegar

1 tablespoon honey

1 teaspoon pomegranate molasses

¼ teaspoon salt

¼ teaspoon black pepper

1. Pat the halloumi slices very dry with a paper towel. Set aside.

2. Heat the oil in a grill pan or a heavy-bottomed skillet over medium heat. Add the sliced halloumi in a single layer. Cook, undisturbed, until the bottoms are golden brown, 3 to 5 minutes. Flip the halloumi and cook until the other side is also golden brown, 2 to 4 minutes longer. Transfer the halloumi to a plate; let cool for at least 10 minutes.

3. Meanwhile, in a small bowl, whisk the oil, vinegar, honey, pomegranate molasses, salt, and pepper. Set aside.

4. On a large serving platter, arrange the lettuce, peaches, onion, walnuts, and grilled halloumi. Drizzle the dressing over the salad and serve immediately.

Cabbage, Cucumber & Sumac Slaw

Serves 6   Active Time: 15 minutes   Total Time: 15 minutes

This salad is a Mediterranean take on coleslaw with its refreshing crunch and tart-bright taste. Here, thinly sliced cabbage is tossed with cucumbers, green onions, and mint for a salad that can wear so many hats. It's the best base for proteins or cooked grains if you'd like to make it a meal, and it's also the perfect any-season side dish for mains like Herby White Bean Burgers (page 168) or Mujadara (page 167). It also keeps really well, so if you'd like to prepare this slaw the night before, go for it! The flavors will only continue to meld—some people like it just as much, if not better, after twenty-four hours.

Dressing

¼ **cup extra-virgin olive oil**

3 **tablespoons lemon juice**

1 **teaspoon ground sumac**

1 **garlic clove,** crushed to a paste

½ **teaspoon salt**

½ **teaspoon black pepper**

Salad

½ **large head of green cabbage,** thinly sliced (about 6 cups)

3 **Persian cucumbers,** thinly sliced

3 **green onions** (whites and greens), thinly sliced

¼ **cup chopped fresh mint**

In a large bowl, whisk the oil, lemon juice, sumac, garlic, salt, and pepper. Add the cabbage, cucumbers, onions, and mint. Toss well to combine and serve immediately.

Warm Roasted Vegetable & Farro Salad

Serves 4   Active Time: 20 minutes   Total Time: 60 minutes

I can eat salads all year round, but in the winter I love adding cozy elements like grilled chicken, roasted vegetables, or cooked whole grains. This warm vegetarian salad is one of my favorites during the colder months, with zaatar-spiced veggies, hearty farro, and a simple-yet-fantastic balsamic vinaigrette. This is a perfect any-occasion dish you need in your back pocket! Bring it to a dinner party or a community potluck or make a big batch at the beginning of the week for easy lunch assembly—this grain salad is always welcome.

Salad

1 cup pearled farro, rinsed and drained

1 eggplant, cut into ½-inch cubes

1 yellow onion, chopped

1 red bell pepper, seeded and chopped

3 tablespoons olive oil

2 teaspoons zaatar

¼ teaspoon salt

¼ teaspoon black pepper

4 cups (packed) **chopped kale leaves**

Dressing

3 tablespoons extra-virgin olive oil

2 tablespoons balsamic vinegar

1 teaspoon pomegranate molasses

1 teaspoon Dijon mustard

¼ teaspoon salt

¼ teaspoon black pepper

1. Bring a small pot of well-salted water to a boil over medium-high heat. Add the farro, stirring once. Return the water to a boil, then reduce the heat to medium-low and cover with a tight-fitting lid. Simmer the farro, stirring occasionally, until tender, about 25 minutes. Drain the farro and set aside.

2. Meanwhile, preheat the oven to 425°F. Line a large baking sheet with parchment paper.

3. Place the eggplant, onion, and bell pepper on the prepared baking sheet. Drizzle everything with the oil and season with the zaatar, salt, and black pepper; toss with your hands until well coated. Spread the vegetables in an even layer and roast, rotating the tray halfway through, until browned and fork-tender, about 45 minutes.

4. Meanwhile, in a large serving bowl, whisk the oil, vinegar, pomegranate molasses, mustard, salt, and pepper. Add the kale; massage the dressing into the kale with your hands until the leaves are tender and well coated.

5. Top the kale with the farro and roasted vegetables. Toss once more to combine and enjoy warm.

Crispy Feta Greek Salad with Zaatar Vinaigrette

Serves 4 | Active Time: 20 minutes | Total Time: 20 minutes

This recipe is inspired by a traditional Greek salad full of thick-cut tomatoes, peppers, cucumbers, and olives. The feta cheese, though, gets a little makeover: it's panfried, crispy, and all kinds of amazing! And instead of using fresh oregano in the salad dressing, I'm using zaatar, my go-to Mediterranean spice blend made with dried wild oregano, sesame seeds, and sumac. So good!

Crispy Feta

1 (8-ounce) **block of feta cheese,** patted dry and cut into ½-inch cubes

¼ cup cornstarch

2 tablespoons extra-virgin olive oil

Dressing

¼ cup extra-virgin olive oil

3 tablespoons lemon juice

1 teaspoon zaatar, plus more for serving

¼ teaspoon salt

Salad

4 Roma tomatoes, chopped

1 green bell pepper, seeded and chopped

2 Persian cucumbers, chopped

½ cup pitted Kalamata olives

1. In a medium bowl, toss the feta with the cornstarch until evenly coated.

2. Heat the oil in a large heavy-bottomed skillet over medium heat. Shake off any excess cornstarch from the feta and add the cubes to the skillet in a single layer. Cook until golden brown, 2 to 4 minutes per side. (The pieces will be a little melty and may not stay in perfect squares—that's fine!) Transfer the crispy feta to a plate. Set aside.

3. In a large serving bowl, whisk the oil, lemon juice, zaatar, and salt. Add the tomatoes, bell pepper, cucumbers, and olives; gently toss everything together. Add the crispy feta on top and sprinkle the salad with more zaatar to taste. Serve immediately.

Sun-Dried Tomato Orzo Salad

Serves 6   Active Time: 15 minutes | Total Time: 25 minutes

Whenever I make this salad, I always get compliments. Everyone wants the recipe for the dressing. The flavor is so delicious and unique, and that comes from the oil that the sun-dried tomatoes are packed in. Many recipes call for draining your oil-packed sun-dried tomatoes, but I say don't throw out the good stuff! It's usually infused with garlic, herbs, and smoky tomato flavor—almost a salad dressing in a jar, if you ask me.

1 cup orzo

4 ounces (about half a 7-ounce jar) **oil-packed julienned sun-dried tomatoes,** oil reserved

1 small shallot, minced

3 tablespoons red wine vinegar

1 teaspoon Dijon mustard

¼ teaspoon salt

¼ teaspoon black pepper

½ cup crumbled feta cheese

½ cup pitted Kalamata olives

1 cup (packed) **arugula**

¼ cup sunflower seeds

1. Bring a large pot of well-salted water to a boil over high heat. Cook the orzo until al dente, according to the package directions. Drain the orzo and run under cold water until cooled.

2. In a large serving bowl, whisk 3 tablespoons of the reserved tomato oil with the shallot, vinegar, mustard, salt, and pepper until emulsified.

3. Transfer the cooled orzo, the tomatoes, feta, olives, and arugula to the bowl with the dressing. Toss to combine. Top the salad with the sunflower seeds. Serve chilled or at room temperature.

Avocado Pesto Pasta Salad

Serves 6 | Active Time: 20 minutes | Total Time: 30 minutes

I'm obsessed with fresh pesto made with simple ingredients to help jump-start easy dinners. This bright green pesto-inspired sauce gets its perfectly creamy texture from ripe avocados. It's not a traditional pesto by any means, but it's a great way to make a deceptively luxurious sauce without adding any extra oil or cream. Just be mindful that, because of the avocado, this is not the kind of pesto you want to freeze. In fact, make sure to eat this salad within twenty-four hours to avoid (harmless but not very pretty) browning—which shouldn't be a problem, I'm sure! One last thing: this delicious pesto is completely vegan, so if you'd like the entire recipe to be vegan just omit the mozzarella.

12 ounces fusilli

2 cups (packed) **fresh basil leaves,** plus more for serving

1 ripe avocado

⅓ cup pine nuts

2 garlic cloves

2 tablespoons lemon juice

¼ teaspoon salt

¼ teaspoon black pepper

3 tablespoons extra-virgin olive oil, plus more for serving

1 pint cherry tomatoes, halved

8 ounces fresh mozzarella pearls or ciliegine, drained

1. Bring a large pot of well-salted water to a boil over high heat. Add the pasta and cook according to the package directions. Drain the pasta and rinse with cold water until completely cool. Transfer to a large serving bowl. Set aside.

2. Meanwhile, place the basil in a food processor and pulse until finely chopped. Add the avocado, pine nuts, garlic, lemon juice, salt, and pepper; pulse to combine. With the food processor running, slowly drizzle in the oil, stopping to scrape down the sides of the bowl as needed, until smooth and creamy.

3. Transfer the avocado pesto to the bowl with the pasta; toss to combine. Fold in the tomatoes and mozzarella. Serve with more basil and a drizzle of oil.

Potato Salad with Fried Capers

Serves 4   Active Time: 20 minutes   Total Time: 30 minutes

I remember the first time I tasted a fried caper. I wondered why I had never thought to fry them before! I love the bright, briny flavor of capers and the texture they add to dishes. But let me tell you: when fried, they might actually be even more amazing. They lose some of their pungency and become crisp, light, and almost nutty. I highly recommend trying them out. (They're fantastic added to basically anything, especially salads, pastas, and meaty mains.) That said, if you don't have time to fry the capers, just add them as-is from the jar—this potato salad will still be delicious!

1½ pounds baby yellow potatoes, quartered

¼ cup capers plus 2 tablespoons caper brine

⅓ cup Greek yogurt

¼ cup chopped fresh dill

2 tablespoons lemon juice

1 tablespoon Dijon mustard

1 small shallot, chopped

1 garlic clove, minced

¼ teaspoon salt

¼ teaspoon black pepper

2 tablespoons extra-virgin olive oil

1. Place the potatoes in a large pot of well-salted water and bring to a boil over high heat. Reduce the heat to medium-low and simmer until the potatoes are fork-tender, about 10 minutes. Drain the potatoes in a colander and run under cold water until cooled. Set aside.

2. In a medium bowl, whisk the caper brine, yogurt, dill, lemon juice, mustard, shallot, garlic, salt, and pepper. Add the potatoes and toss gently to combine.

3. Pat the capers as dry as possible with paper towels. Heat the oil in a small nonstick skillet over medium heat. Add the capers and fry until darkened and crisp, 3 to 5 minutes. Sprinkle the fried capers and any leftover fried caper oil over the potato salad.

Pomegranate Green Bean Salad

Serves 4 | Active Time: 15 minutes | Total Time: 15 minutes

Here's the great thing about this green bean salad: it's full of crunch without having to use any leafy greens. I mean, I love leafy greens, but this salad is great for when you need a break from lettuce. You'll also get an extra-satisfying crunch from the pomegranate seeds, which top this salad like little gems. Their red hue contrasted with the green beans is beautiful enough for any occasion but still simple enough to whip up on a weekday to enjoy with my Lemony Grilled Chicken Kabobs (page 205).

Salad

1 pound green beans, trimmed and cut into 2-inch pieces

¼ **cup sliced almonds**

¼ **cup pomegranate seeds**

Dressing

½ **shallot,** minced

3 tablespoons red wine vinegar

1 teaspoon pomegranate molasses

¼ **teaspoon salt**

¼ **teaspoon black pepper**

¼ **cup extra-virgin olive oil**

1. Bring a large pot of well-salted water to a boil over high heat. Meanwhile, prepare a medium bowl filled with ice water.

2. Add the green beans to the boiling water. Cook until tender and bright green, 3 to 4 minutes. Drain the green beans in a colander and transfer to the ice bath. Chill for 5 minutes. Drain the green beans once more and pat dry with a paper towel.

3. In a large serving bowl, whisk the shallot, vinegar, pomegranate molasses, salt, and pepper. Whisking constantly, slowly stream in the oil until smooth and well blended. Add the green beans and toss to combine. Top with the almonds and pomegranate seeds.

4

Sandwiches & Soups

Tahini & Smashed Avocado Chicken Sandwich

Serves 4 | Active Time: 20 minutes | Total Time: 20 minutes

When I was growing up, chicken sandwiches consisted of chicken shawarma sandwiches and chicken tawook sandwiches, with tahini sauce or garlic sauce. This sandwich is a nod to my childhood chicken sandwich days but in a reimagined way: with thick slices of ciabatta and loads of avocado, arugula, and sun-dried tomatoes. It's colorful, it's nutritious, and it's the sandwich you need in your life ASAP.

1 pound chicken cutlets or boneless, skinless chicken breasts, halved lengthwise

1 teaspoon paprika

1 teaspoon garlic powder

¾ teaspoon salt, divided

½ teaspoon black pepper

3 tablespoons olive oil, divided

½ cup Greek yogurt

⅓ cup tahini

¼ cup lemon juice

1 loaf of ciabatta, halved lengthwise

1 avocado, mashed

¼ cup oil-packed julienned sun-dried tomatoes, drained

1 cup arugula

1. Rub the chicken with the paprika, garlic powder, ½ teaspoon of the salt, the pepper, and 2 tablespoons of the oil. Heat the remaining 1 tablespoon of oil in a grill pan or large nonstick skillet over medium-high heat. Grill or sear the chicken, flipping once, until lightly charred and cooked through, 8 to 10 minutes total. Remove the chicken from the heat and tent with foil to keep it warm.

2. In a small bowl, whisk the yogurt, tahini, lemon juice, and the remaining ¼ teaspoon of salt until smooth.

3. Spread the yogurt-tahini sauce on the bottom and top halves of the ciabatta. Top the bottom half of the ciabatta with the avocado, tomatoes, chicken, and arugula, then add the top half of the ciabatta. Slice the sandwich into 4 pieces and enjoy immediately.

Crispy Spinach & Feta Grilled Cheese

Serves 2 | Active Time: 15 minutes | Total Time: 15 minutes

I always love adding a serving of vegetables whenever I can. And there's nothing easier to sneak into a sandwich than a bunch of cooked spinach, if you ask me! I mean, spinach does this crazy magical number where it practically disappears when you cook it in a skillet. This might be a bummer if you were looking to feed a group more than a thimbleful of spinach, but it's a total win if you're looking to add some nutritious and neutral-tasting greens to your sandwich. The pop of color comes with some great added health benefits, and as for the grilled cheese—who needs to be sold on grilled cheese?

3 tablespoons salted butter, divided

5 cups (packed) **baby spinach** (about 5 ounces)

¼ cup fresh basil, chopped

½ cup crumbled feta cheese

1 garlic clove, minced

½ teaspoon ground cumin

Salt and black pepper

4 slices of sourdough bread

1 cup shredded low-moisture mozzarella cheese

1. Melt 1 tablespoon of the butter in a large skillet over medium heat. Add the spinach and cook, stirring frequently, until the spinach begins to wilt, 1 to 2 minutes. Add the basil, feta, garlic, and cumin. Stir until the feta is warmed through and starting to melt, about 2 minutes. Season to taste with the salt and pepper and transfer the mixture to a small bowl. Set aside.

2. Wipe the skillet clean. Melt 1 tablespoon of the butter over medium heat, swirling to coat the pan. Place 2 slices of the bread in the skillet. Divide half of the mozzarella between both pieces of bread (about ¼ cup each), then evenly top with the spinach mixture. Divide the rest of the mozzarella on top, then close each sandwich with the remaining 2 slices of bread.

3. Cook the sandwiches on one side until the bread is golden and crispy, 3 to 5 minutes. Just before you're ready to flip them, melt the remaining 1 tablespoon of butter in the skillet. Carefully flip the sandwiches and cook until the other side is golden brown and the cheese is melty, 2 to 4 minutes longer. Cut the sandwiches in half and serve immediately.

Sumac-Spiced Hummus & Veggie Pitas

Serves 4 | Active Time: 15 minutes | Total Time: 15 minutes

Sandwiches are more fun as pockets! Sometimes, I forgo my usual Arabic-style pita and instead opt for Greek-style pita with its thick, plush texture and deep pockets. These pita pockets are perfect for stuffing with dips and vegetables for a quick, satisfying, and filling lunch. Pro tip: Warm the pitas up a little before you slice and stuff them—this will make them more pliable and less prone to tearing. This sandwich is basically a handheld salad, which is great if you're in a salad rut, you want to up your intake of veggies, or if your kids are on a salad strike. This recipe calls for Baba's Classic Hummus (page 66), but store-bought is totally fine in a pinch.

4 Greek-style pitas

1 cup Baba's Classic Hummus (page 66)

1 teaspoon ground sumac

1 teaspoon dried oregano

1 cup chopped romaine lettuce

1 Roma tomato, sliced

½ English cucumber, sliced

½ avocado, sliced

¼ cup thinly sliced red onion

Salt and black pepper

1. Slice each pita in half and open up the pita pockets. Divide the hummus between the 8 pockets, spreading evenly on both sides. Sprinkle the hummus with the sumac and oregano.

2. Evenly divide the lettuce, tomato, cucumber, avocado, and onion between the 8 pockets. Season to taste with the salt and pepper and serve immediately.

Mediterranean-Style Tuna Wrap

Serves 4 | Active Time: 15 minutes | Total Time: 15 minutes

Tuna salad is an easy go-to lunch for me, and it's usually tucked into a wrap or sandwiched between two slices of toasted bread. To make my tuna salad a little lighter and to add a nice boost of protein, I use Greek yogurt instead of mayonnaise. The yogurt adds a wonderfully creamy texture and subtle tang when mixed with Dijon mustard and dill—and it's honestly hard to tell it's not mayonnaise. The fresh lemon and capers give this classic tuna salad a light Mediterranean spin that's hard not to love. And the bright and tangy Pickled Red Onions (page 253) give it a pop of color and a taste that's perfect with tuna.

½ **lemon**

⅓ **cup Greek yogurt**

1 tablespoon **Dijon mustard**

1 tablespoon chopped **fresh dill**

2 (5-ounce) **cans albacore tuna in water,** drained

2 **celery stalks,** minced

2 tablespoons **capers,** drained

Salt and black pepper

2 cups (packed) **baby spinach**

4 (10-inch) **soft flour tortillas**

1 cup **Pickled Red Onions** (page 253)

1. Zest and juice the lemon into a small bowl. Stir in the yogurt, mustard, and dill until well combined. Add the tuna, celery, and capers and use a fork to mash it all together. Season to taste with the salt and pepper and stir until everything is incorporated.

2. Evenly divide the spinach between each tortilla, piling it into the center. Divide the tuna salad on top of the spinach, and add the pickled onions on top. Fold one side of the first tortilla over the salad, tuck in the ends, and then roll firmly to make a wrap. Repeat with the remaining tortillas. Slice each tortilla in half diagonally and serve immediately.

Open-Faced Labneh & Zaatar Sandwich

Serves 4　|　Active Time: 10 minutes　|　Total Time: 20 minutes

Growing up, I ate a lot of sandwiches either wrapped in Arabic pita or stuffed between two toasted slices of French bread. And though my house now is never without pita, French bread takes a close second as one of my more nostalgic mealtime staples. As a kid, I used to eat these zaatar-loaded sandwiches with plenty of labneh, and this recipe is a nod to the classic version I grew up on. It's one of those sandwiches I ate for breakfast, lunch, snacks, and even dinner at times. So, when I say, "grew up on," I do mean literally—I am probably 60 percent open-faced labneh and zaatar sandwich at this point.

⅓ cup **zaatar**

¼ cup **extra-virgin olive oil**

½ **loaf of French bread** (about 8 ounces), cut in half lengthwise

½ cup **Labneh** (page 258)

¼ **English cucumber,** thinly sliced

2 tablespoons **fresh mint leaves,** torn

1. Preheat the oven to 400°F. Line a baking sheet with parchment paper.

2. In a small bowl, mix the zaatar with the oil until it forms a spreadable paste. Place the 2 bread halves on the prepared baking sheet. Spread the zaatar mixture evenly over the cut sides. Bake the bread cut side up until the edges are beginning to turn crisp and golden brown, about 10 minutes. Transfer the bread to a cutting board and let cool for 5 minutes.

3. Cut both pieces of the bread in quarters crosswise. Spread the labneh evenly on top of each slice, then top with the cucumber and scatter with the mint.

Caprese Grilled Pitas

Serves 4   Active Time: 15 minutes   Total Time: 15 minutes

Since I only eat halal meat, finding suitable sandwiches when I go out to eat can be tricky. I often fall back on a classic grilled tomato-and-mozzarella-stuffed sandwich because it's both popular and vegetarian. My ideal grilled caprese, though, is one I make at home, stuffed into a pita and pressed into melty, crispy perfection. It makes me wonder: why aren't all these kinds of sandwiches made on pita instead of, like, sourdough? I mean, you can't beat the cheese-to-bread ratio in pita—the best thing in my book!

4 Greek-style pitas

8 tablespoons pesto

8 ounces fresh mozzarella, cut into ¼-inch slices

2 Roma tomatoes, cut into ¼-inch slices

½ cup (loosely packed) **fresh basil**

¼ teaspoon salt

¼ teaspoon black pepper

2 tablespoons olive oil, divided

1. Slice each pita in half and open up the pita pockets. Divide the pesto between the 8 pockets, spreading evenly on both sides. Divide the mozzarella, tomatoes, and basil between each pocket and season with the salt and pepper.

2. Heat 1 tablespoon of the oil in a grill pan or large nonstick skillet over medium heat. Add 4 stuffed pita halves. Cook on one side, undisturbed, until the pitas are lightly browned with char marks, 3 to 5 minutes. Carefully flip the pitas, pressing down with the back of a spatula, until the second side is browned and the cheese is melty, 2 to 4 minutes longer. Repeat with the remaining 1 tablespoon oil and 4 stuffed pita halves. Serve immediately.

Chicken Vermicelli Soup

Serves 6   Active Time: 30 minutes   Total Time: 1 hour

There's nothing more comforting than chicken noodle soup, and for me the nostalgia is in the noodles. I can spot a Lebanese chicken noodle soup from a mile away because we use vermicelli pasta. These extra-thin noodles help thicken the soup without taking the spotlight away from the chicken and vegetables. I mean, vermicelli is even thinner than angel hair pasta! And if you can't find vermicelli, angel hair pasta is actually a great substitute—just use your hands to break it into smaller one-inch pieces before adding it to the soup.

2 tablespoons olive oil

1 yellow onion, diced

3 large carrots, diced

3 celery stalks, diced

1 teaspoon salt, divided

1 teaspoon black pepper, divided

3 garlic cloves, minced

1 teaspoon dried oregano

1½ pounds bone-in chicken breasts

2 dried bay leaves

¾ cup vermicelli

2 tablespoons chopped fresh parsley

2 tablespoons lemon juice

1. Heat the oil in a large stockpot over medium heat. Add the onion, carrots, celery, ½ teaspoon of the salt, and ½ teaspoon of the pepper. Cook, stirring occasionally, until softened, about 10 minutes.

2. Add the garlic and oregano. Cook, stirring constantly, until fragrant, about 1 minute. Add the chicken and bay leaves and season with the remaining ½ teaspoon of salt and ½ teaspoon of pepper.

3. Add 6 cups of water, making sure the chicken is just covered with the liquid. Bring everything to a boil over medium-high heat. Reduce the heat to medium-low and simmer, covered, until the chicken is cooked through, about 25 minutes.

4. Transfer the cooked chicken to a cutting board. Using two forks, shred the chicken from the bones into bite-size pieces, discarding the bones. Return the shredded chicken to the soup along with the vermicelli. Continue to cook the soup over medium-low heat until the pasta is tender, about 5 minutes. Remove the soup from the heat and stir in the parsley and lemon juice.

Roasted Tomato Soup with Labneh

Serves 6 | Active Time: 15 minutes | Total Time: 60 minutes

Sometimes, to switch things up when making soup, I like tossing vegetables and aromatics onto a baking sheet to roast instead of standing over a stockpot. That hands-off spirit is exactly what I use to make this roasted tomato soup. Even better, roasting sweetens and caramelizes the tomatoes, which release delicious flavors and juices that end up mingling with slowly softening garlic, onion, and fresh rosemary—a huge boost of flavor that's achieved without breaking out the wooden spoon for sautéing. This soup is delicious on its own with creamy-tart labneh blended in, but don't sleep on pairing it with my Crispy Spinach & Feta Grilled Cheese (page 128), either!

4 pounds ripe Roma tomatoes, halved

1 large yellow onion, chopped

6 garlic cloves

2 tablespoons fresh rosemary leaves

¼ cup extra-virgin olive oil, plus more for serving

¼ teaspoon crushed red pepper

1 teaspoon salt

1 teaspoon black pepper

4 cups vegetable broth

½ cup (packed) **fresh basil leaves,** plus more for serving

½ cup Labneh (page 258), plus more for serving

1. Preheat the oven to 425°F. Line a large baking sheet with parchment paper.

2. On the baking sheet, gently mix the tomatoes, onion, garlic, rosemary, oil, crushed red pepper, salt, and black pepper. Spread everything out in a single layer and arrange the tomatoes cut side down. Roast until tender and caramelized, about 45 minutes.

3. Transfer the contents of the baking sheet (including any liquid) to a large pot and add the broth. Bring the mixture to a boil over high heat and then immediately remove the pot from the heat. Stir in the basil and labneh.

4. Use an immersion blender to blend the soup until smooth and creamy. Ladle soup into 6 bowls and garnish with the labneh, basil, and olive oil.

Spring Orzo & Pea Soup

Serves 6 | Active Time: 20 minutes | Total Time: 50 minutes

I eat soup all year long, even when the weather gets warmer. When the ice finally thaws in Michigan and we get that first batch of mild spring days, I celebrate with this recipe— it's packed with bright, sunshiny flavors like fresh herbs, citrus, and green vegetables, fresh or frozen. You can easily have this soup as an appetizer before your main course at a dinner party (how fancy!), but I also love enjoying a hot bowl as a whole meal. Thanks to the protein in those peas and the filling orzo, this soup is so satisfying, nourishing, and delicious.

2 tablespoons (¼ stick) **salted butter**

1 yellow onion, chopped

3 celery stalks, chopped

¾ teaspoon salt

½ teaspoon black pepper

2 garlic cloves, minced

½ cup orzo

½ cup chopped fresh dill, plus more for serving

2 cups frozen peas

6 cups vegetable broth

1 lime

Grated Parmesan cheese, for serving

1. Melt the butter in a large stockpot over medium heat. Add the onion, celery, salt, and pepper. Cook, stirring occasionally, until tender, about 10 minutes.

2. Stir in the garlic and cook, stirring constantly, until fragrant, 30 seconds to 1 minute.

3. Add the orzo, dill, peas, and broth. Bring everything to a boil, then reduce the heat to medium-low. Simmer, covered, until the orzo is cooked through and becomes visibly plump, about 20 minutes.

4. Remove the pot from the heat. Zest and juice the lime into the soup. Serve with the Parmesan and more dill.

Lemony Chickpea Pasta Soup

Serves 6 | Active Time: 20 minutes | Total Time: 50 minutes

As much as I love me some chicken soup (see Chicken Vermicelli Soup and Healing Couscous Chicken Soup, pages 139 and 147), I'll just as often forgo any meat and swap in some chickpeas instead. Chickpeas add a satisfying texture and boost of protein to soups and stews. This plant-based soup is velvety, nourishing, veggie-packed, and bright with fresh lemon. Basically, a cozy blanket fit for any and every season.

2 tablespoons olive oil

1 large yellow onion, chopped

3 carrots, chopped

3 celery stalks, chopped

1 teaspoon salt

½ teaspoon black pepper

2 garlic cloves, sliced

4 sprigs of fresh thyme, stemmed

8 cups vegetable broth

2 (15-ounce) **cans chickpeas,** drained and rinsed

8 ounces orecchiette

1 lemon

¼ cup chopped fresh parsley, plus more for serving

1. Heat the oil in a large heavy-bottomed pot over medium heat. Add the onion, carrots, celery, salt, and pepper. Cook, stirring occasionally, until the vegetables are softened, about 10 minutes.

2. Add the garlic and thyme. Cook, stirring constantly, until very fragrant, about 1 minute. Add the broth and bring everything to a boil over high heat. Reduce the heat to medium-low and simmer for 10 minutes.

3. Use an immersion blender to blend the soup until smooth.

4. Stir in the chickpeas and orecchiette and bring everything to a boil once more over medium-high heat. Cook, stirring occasionally, until the pasta is al dente, about 10 minutes.

5. Remove the soup from the heat. Zest and juice the lemon into the pot and then stir in the parsley. Serve with more parsley sprinkled on top.

Healing Couscous Chicken Soup

Serves 6 | Active Time: 25 minutes | Total Time: 55 minutes

Whenever I feel like I'm getting sick, my mom never fails to tell me that her favorite home remedy is chicken noodle soup. But this is not your traditional chicken noodle soup. (For that, you can check out my Chicken Vermicelli Soup, page 139—a Lebanese classic!) Here, the chicken actually plays a supporting role to the medicinal properties of ginger, garlic, and turmeric. I start with these nourishing flavors as a base and then add onions and frozen mixed vegetables—because who has the energy to chop tons of vegetables when they're sick? (In the same spirit, it's nice to just buy cooked chicken from the grocery store, which I call for here, but feel free to cook it yourself.) I also bulk up this soup with some kind of easy-to-digest starch like rice or, in this case, pearl couscous. The warmth, aroma, taste, and nutritional value of this soup really does work wonders to make me feel good every time. My dad even makes a ginger, garlic, and turmeric hot drink that he swears by as a cure-all, but I draw the line at drinking garlic!

2 tablespoons olive oil

1 large yellow onion, diced

1 teaspoon salt, divided

½ teaspoon black pepper, divided

1 (16-ounce) bag frozen mixed vegetables (such as carrots, peas, and corn)

3 garlic cloves, minced

1 (1-inch) piece of fresh ginger, minced

2 teaspoons ground turmeric

½ teaspoon ground cumin

½ cup chopped fresh cilantro, divided

1 cup pearl couscous

2 cups diced cooked chicken breasts (from about 2 breasts)

8 cups chicken broth

1. Heat the oil in a large heavy-bottomed pot over medium heat. Add the onion, ½ teaspoon of the salt, and ¼ teaspoon of the pepper. Cook, stirring occasionally, until softened, 5 to 8 minutes.

2. Add the mixed vegetables, and season again with the remaining ½ teaspoon of salt and ¼ teaspoon of pepper. Cook, stirring occasionally, until the vegetables are thawed and any liquid has reduced, 2 to 3 minutes longer.

3. Add the garlic, ginger, turmeric, cumin, and ¼ cup of the cilantro. Cook, stirring constantly, until very fragrant, about 1 minute. Add the couscous, chicken, and broth. Bring everything to a boil over medium-high heat.

4. Reduce the heat to medium-low and simmer, covered, for 30 minutes. Remove the soup from heat. Stir in the remaining ¼ cup of cilantro.

Crushed Lentil Soup

Serves 6 | Active Time: 15 minutes | Total Time: 45 minutes

This red lentil soup is arguably the most popular one in the Middle East. It can be made with as few as four ingredients: olive oil, onions, red lentils, and cumin. But I love making this iconic soup heartier by adding short-grain rice, carrots, and a big burst of lemon juice and fresh parsley to finish. Crushed lentil soup is often made during the fasting month of Ramadan to break the daily fast with something nutritious, delicious, and heartwarming. You'll also find it on all Lebanese restaurant menus if you're lucky enough to have a great spot nearby. It's relatively quick, naturally vegan, and a nice reminder not to underestimate the power of a few humble ingredients.

1 tablespoon olive oil

1 yellow onion, chopped

1 teaspoon salt, divided

½ teaspoon black pepper, divided

2 carrots, chopped

1½ cups red lentils, rinsed and drained

½ cup short-grain white rice, rinsed

2 teaspoons ground cumin

Juice of 1 lemon

Chopped fresh parsley, for garnish

1. Heat the oil in a large heavy-bottomed pot over medium heat. Add the onion, ½ teaspoon of the salt, and ¼ teaspoon of the pepper. Cook, stirring occasionally, until softened, 5 to 8 minutes.

2. Add the carrots, lentils, rice, and cumin. Season again with the remaining ½ teaspoon of salt and ¼ teaspoon of pepper. Cook, stirring frequently, until the cumin is fragrant, 2 to 3 minutes.

3. Add 8 cups of water and bring the soup to a boil over high heat. Reduce the heat to low and cook, covered, stirring once or twice throughout, until the rice and lentils are fluffy and fully cooked, 25 to 30 minutes.

4. Using an immersion blender, pulse the soup a few times for a coarse-yet-creamy consistency. (If you don't have an immersion blender, you can skip this step.) The soup will continue to thicken as it sits. Stir in the lemon juice and chopped fresh parsley before serving.

Kafta & Potato Soup

Serves 6 | Active Time: 25 minutes | Total Time: 1 hour

Kafta patties and sliced potatoes stewed or baked in a gently spiced tomato sauce is such a delicious dish, and my kids also go crazy for it. One day I had the idea to expand my love for this meal into a cozy, soul-warming soup. Now, when the weather begins to drop each year, I quickly turn to this recipe. Although it's inspired by kafta patties, I skip the extra step of forming the kafta by hand while keeping all of the same flavors. (Feel free to try my Tahini Kafta, page 214, if you're craving a more classic version!) Seriously, this soup is so good, so simple, and so perfect for chilly days.

2 teaspoons olive oil

1 yellow onion, diced

1 pound lean ground beef

1 teaspoon salt

½ teaspoon black pepper

¼ cup chopped fresh parsley, plus more for serving

2 teaspoons Seven Spice (page 259 or store-bought)

1 teaspoon ground cumin

1 teaspoon ground coriander

½ teaspoon ground cinnamon

4 medium Yukon gold potatoes, peeled and diced

1 green bell pepper, seeded and diced

1 (14-ounce) can tomato sauce

1 (14-ounce) can diced tomatoes

4 cups vegetable broth

1. Heat the oil in a large pot over medium heat. Add the onion, beef, salt, and black pepper. Cook, stirring occasionally to break up the beef, until the onion is soft and the beef is browned, 8 to 10 minutes. Add the parsley, seven spice, cumin, coriander, and cinnamon and stir until fragrant, about 30 seconds.

2. Add the potatoes and bell pepper and stir. Pour in the tomato sauce, diced tomatoes, and broth and stir again.

3. Bring everything to a boil over medium-high heat, then reduce the heat to medium-low and simmer, uncovered, until the potatoes are tender, 35 to 40 minutes. Remove the soup from heat. Stir in more parsley and serve.

Farro Mushroom Soup

Serves 6 | Active Time: 30 minutes | Total Time: 1 hour

If you're familiar with cream of mushroom soup, you know how delicious, rich, and hearty it can be. I absolutely love the flavor, but since it always tends to leave me feeling uncomfortably full, I made some tweaks over the years. I bumped up the vegetables, reduced the cream, and added satisfying whole-grain farro to give it more body and nutrients. The result is one fantastic soup, if I do say so myself. It's one of the first soups I begin to crave when the months get colder.

2 tablespoons olive oil

1 large yellow onion, finely chopped

2 celery stalks, thinly sliced

1 teaspoon salt, divided

½ teaspoon black pepper, divided

1 cup pearled farro, rinsed and drained

1 pound mixed mushrooms, thinly sliced

3 garlic cloves, minced

2 tablespoons chopped fresh rosemary

2 teaspoons dried oregano

6 cups vegetable broth

½ cup heavy cream

½ cup grated Parmesan cheese, plus more for serving

1 tablespoon balsamic vinegar

1. Heat the oil in a large heavy-bottomed pot over medium heat. Add the onion, celery, ½ teaspoon of the salt, and ¼ teaspoon of the pepper. Cook, stirring occasionally, until the onion is softened, about 10 minutes. Add the farro and toast, stirring frequently, for about 2 minutes.

2. Add the mushrooms, garlic, rosemary, oregano, and the remaining ½ teaspoon of salt and ¼ teaspoon of pepper. Cook, stirring occasionally, until the mushrooms have released their liquid and begin to brown, 6 to 8 minutes. Add the broth and bring everything to a boil over high heat.

3. Reduce the heat to medium-low and simmer, covered, for 30 minutes. Remove the soup from heat. Stirring constantly, gradually pour in the cream. Stir in the Parmesan and vinegar. Serve the soup topped with more Parmesan.

5

Vegetarian Mains

Crispy Falafel

Makes 36 falafel | Active Time: 40 minutes | Total Time: 1 hour and 40 minutes (plus overnight soaking)

There's only one thing I really fry in my house and that's falafel. Air frying or baking falafel just doesn't cut it for me. Only frying in oil creates that perfect texture: crispy edges with super fluffy interiors. So good! And while frying is a huge part of making sure the recipe tastes authentic, using the right kind of chickpeas is more important. Don't even think about using canned chickpeas—since they're cooked, they contain too much moisture, meaning you'll need flour to get the right consistency, meaning your falafel will be dense. You have to start with dry, uncooked chickpeas. I know, I know. There's nothing I love more than a shortcut, too, but the best falafel requires the scenic route. This is also why, although every recipe in this book is at most thirty minutes of active time, these falafel take forty minutes. Nothing here is hard, it's just precise, and I've already done all the organizing for you down to the minutes and teaspoons. Believe me, it's all so worth it! Want to make perfect falafel at home? This is how.

1 pound dry, uncooked chickpeas

1 tablespoon salt

¾ cup fresh parsley

½ cup fresh cilantro

1 large yellow onion, roughly chopped

1 garlic clove

2 teaspoons ground cumin

2 teaspoons ground coriander

1 teaspoon black pepper

1 teaspoon baking powder

Neutral oil, such as canola oil, for frying

Tahini Sauce (page 256)

1. In a medium bowl, cover the chickpeas with water. Set aside at room temperature to soak for at least 12 or up to 24 hours.

2. Drain the chickpeas. Rinse and dry them well.

3. Place the chickpeas and salt in a food processor. Pulse to fine pebble-size pieces. Add the parsley, cilantro, onion, garlic, cumin, coriander, and pepper. Blend until the mixture turns into a thick paste, scraping down the sides as needed. Remove the blade from the bowl, then cover the bowl of the food processor and refrigerate for 1 hour (this allows the batter to set).

4. Remove the falafel batter from the fridge. Sprinkle the baking powder over the top, then gently fold it throughout.

5. Line a large baking sheet with parchment paper and another large baking sheet with a double layer of paper towels. Set aside.

6. Using a medium spring-loaded cookie scoop or your hands, scoop, firmly pack, and roll about 1½ tablespoons of batter into a ball and add it to the parchment paper–lined baking sheet. Repeat with the remaining batter. Don't worry if the balls feel a little loose at first—they will bind once they fry.

7. Heat 1 inch of the oil in a large high-sided frying pan over medium heat. When a small piece of batter dropped into the oil begins to sizzle, carefully add 10 to 12 of the balls, being careful not to crowd the pan. Fry until golden brown and crispy, 3 to 3½ minutes per side. Using a slotted spoon, transfer the cooked falafel to the paper towel–lined baking sheet. Repeat with the remaining uncooked falafel.

8. Transfer the falafel to a serving platter alongside the Tahini Sauce for dipping.

Baked Feta Pasta

Serves 4 | Active Time: 15 minutes | Total Time: 50 minutes

Oh, baked feta pasta. Baked feta pasta! This creamy, savory, absolutely delicious recipe started in Finland, and when a blogger made it in the United States, I decided to give it a try myself, with a couple of tweaks. Well, I made it go viral, with tens of millions of views on my website and social media. I heard some supermarkets even ran out of feta cheese! I was featured in Vogue *and the* New York Times. *In short: this dish has kinda become my claim to fame. I love that it showcases an intriguing way to enjoy feta (my MVP) and how sophisticated yet simple it feels. How could I share my favorite Mediterranean recipes in this book without it?*

2 pints cherry tomatoes

½ cup extra-virgin olive oil

¼ teaspoon salt

¼ teaspoon black pepper

1 (8-ounce) **block of feta cheese**

8 ounces cavatappi

2 garlic cloves, minced

¼ cup (packed) **chopped fresh basil,** plus more for serving

1. Preheat the oven to 400°F.

2. Place the cherry tomatoes in an 8 × 11-inch baking dish. Add the oil, salt, and pepper; toss everything together. Nestle the block of feta in the middle of the baking dish. Gently flip it a couple of times to coat it with the oil and seasonings. Bake until the tomatoes have burst and the feta is melty and bubbly, about 35 minutes.

3. Meanwhile, bring a large pot of well-salted water to a boil over high heat. Cook the pasta until al dente, according to the package directions. Drain the pasta and set aside.

4. When the feta-tomato mixture is ready, add the garlic and basil. Using a fork, carefully mash everything together until well combined. Transfer the cooked pasta to the feta sauce, tossing until well coated. Garnish with more basil and serve warm.

Rigatoni with Pistachio-Basil Sauce

Serves 4 | Active Time: 15 minutes | Total Time: 25 minutes

This bright green pistachio-basil sauce is the perfect way to use up fresh basil at the end of the summer when it's overtaking gardens across the Midwest. I add a generous handful of spinach for a satisfying boost of vitamins and fiber and shelled pistachios for a buttery finish—and because I always seem to have more pistachios than I need at any given time. This recipe is pretty versatile, so feel free to sub in pine nuts, almonds, or walnuts instead. (Those nuts that are going stale in your pantry? This is their time!)

1 cup (packed) **fresh basil leaves,** plus more for garnish

1 cup (packed) **spinach**

⅓ cup shelled pistachios

3 garlic cloves

Zest and juice of 1 small lemon

½ cup grated Parmesan cheese, divided

½ cup extra-virgin olive oil

Salt and black pepper

12 ounces rigatoni

2 tablespoons (¼ stick) **salted butter**

1. In a food processor, pulse the basil, spinach, pistachios, garlic, lemon zest, lemon juice, and ¼ cup of the Parmesan. With the machine running, slowly stream in the oil. Process until smooth and creamy. Season to taste with the salt and pepper.

2. Bring a large pot of well-salted water to a boil over high heat. Cook the pasta until al dente, according to the package directions. Reserve ½ cup of the pasta cooking water, then drain the pasta.

3. Return the pasta to the pot along with the basil-pistachio sauce. Add the reserved pasta water, the remaining ¼ cup of Parmesan, and the butter. Cook over medium-high heat, stirring frequently, until the sauce is thickened and glossy, 1 to 3 minutes. Serve immediately.

Spaghetti with Garlicky Yogurt Sauce

Serves 4 | Active Time: 15 minutes | Total Time: 25 minutes

Macarona bi laban, an Arabic dish of cooked pasta tossed in a glossy, garlicky yogurt sauce, was kind of like our version of pasta Alfredo growing up. Some cooks pour the cold sauce right over the cooked pasta, but I like to warm everything up a bit in the pot before serving—it mellows out the minced raw garlic and creates a silky-smooth texture that clings to the pasta perfectly. You'll note that I use plain yogurt here, not Greek, which is an intentional choice for the best texture. (If you only have the latter on hand, that's fine, though.) You'll also notice that I boost this recipe with a hint of tahini, which adds a gentle but satisfying savoriness that I can't get enough of. If you'd like to bulk things up even more, try this pasta topped with a few generous spoonfuls of hashweh— it's a very common way to enjoy it.

8 ounces spaghetti

2 tablespoons olive oil

2 tablespoons pine nuts

3 garlic cloves, minced

1 cup plain whole-milk yogurt

1 tablespoon tahini

½ teaspoon salt

2 tablespoons chopped fresh parsley

Hashweh (optional; page 217)

1. Bring a large pot of well-salted water to a boil over high heat. Cook the pasta until al dente, according to package directions. Reserve ¼ cup of the pasta cooking water, then drain the pasta and set aside.

2. Heat the oil in a large skillet over medium heat. Add the pine nuts. Cook, stirring frequently, until fragrant and golden brown, 2 to 4 minutes. Using a slotted spoon, transfer the pine nuts into a small bowl and set aside.

3. Remove the skillet from the heat. Stir the garlic into the warm oil until fragrant, about 30 seconds. Add the yogurt, tahini, and salt and whisk until everything is smooth and creamy.

4. Add the cooked pasta and the reserved pasta water to the skillet with the sauce. Place the skillet over medium heat and cook, tossing constantly, until the sauce is thickened, glossy, and clinging to the pasta, 1 to 2 minutes longer. Scatter with the toasted pine nuts and the parsley. Serve immediately with the Hashweh spooned over top (if using).

Quinoa, Feta & White Bean Bowl

Serves 4 | Active Time: 20 minutes | Total Time: 35 minutes

One of the best ways to repurpose leftovers is with satisfying grain bowls because anything goes! It's the ultimate blank canvas and a great vehicle for fitting healthy things like produce and protein into mealtimes. This recipe is one that I threw together on a whim one day with a few things lingering in my fridge and pantry, and wow, what a fresh and wonderful surprise. I now go out of my way to make this bowl routinely—the hearty mixed grains, tangy cheese, creamy beans, and fresh greens really hit the spot. The only thing you're cooking here is the quinoa, and I like to cook it in vegetable broth for extra flavor.

1½ **cups quinoa**

2¼ **cups vegetable broth**

¼ **teaspoon salt**

¼ **teaspoon black pepper**

1 (15-ounce) **can white beans,** drained and rinsed

2 **cups** (packed) **arugula**

1 **cup crumbled feta cheese**

1 **cup Pickled Red Onions** (page 253)

½ **cup shelled pistachios,** chopped

¼ **cup chopped fresh dill**

½ **cup Tahini Sauce** (page 256), for drizzling

1. Rinse the quinoa in a fine-mesh sieve under cold water until the water runs clear.

2. Transfer the quinoa to a small saucepan with a fitted lid. Add the broth, salt, and pepper and bring to a boil over high heat. Reduce the heat to medium-low and continue to cook, covered, for 20 minutes. Remove the pot from the heat and let stand, covered, for 5 minutes.

3. Fluff the quinoa with a fork and divide it into four bowls. Divide the beans, arugula, feta, Pickled Red Onions, pistachios, and dill on top. Drizzle each bowl with the Tahini Sauce and serve.

Mujadara

Serves 8 | Active Time: 30 minutes | Total Time: 1 hour 25 minutes

Mujadara is a classic Arabic dish of cooked lentils and rice scented with a little cumin and topped with savory-sweet caramelized and crispy onions. It's one of my favorite meals my mom made growing up, and I appreciate this humble dish just as much to this day: it's inexpensive, nutritious, filling, and so, so good. Mujadara is truly greater than the sum of its parts, and, though simple, the preparation is quite specific. The best part of the recipe is the crispy onions on top, so make sure to crank up the heat to high and stir constantly to get beautiful, even browning. The feel and flavor of this dish is seriously one of the coziest comfort foods around.

1 cup long-grain white rice

½ cup olive oil

2 large yellow onions, thinly sliced

2 cups brown lentils, rinsed and drained

1 teaspoon salt

2 teaspoons ground cumin

Cucumber Yogurt Sauce (optional; page 257)

1. In a medium bowl, cover the rice with cold water. Set aside.

2. Line a plate with two paper towels. Heat the oil in a large pot over high heat. Add the onions and cook, stirring frequently, until they're deeply browned and start to crisp around the edges, about 20 minutes. Transfer to the prepared plate and set aside. They will continue to crisp as they cool.

3. In a different large pot, bring 4½ cups of water to a boil over high heat. Stir in the lentils. Return the water to a boil, then reduce the heat to medium-low and cover with a tight-fitting lid. Cook for 15 minutes.

4. Drain the soaked rice and transfer it to the pot with the lentils. Add the salt, stir once, then cover again and cook undisturbed for 15 minutes. Remove the pot from the heat. Rest, covered, for 5 minutes longer.

5. Add the cumin and fluff the rice and lentils with a fork to combine. Spoon the crispy onions on top of the mujadara. Serve warm with the Cucumber Yogurt Sauce (if using).

Herby White Bean Burgers

Serves 4 | Active Time: 25 minutes | Total Time: 25 minutes

This recipe is fantastic whether you're vegetarian or simply trying to include more meatless proteins at mealtimes. It's loaded with satisfying protein and fiber from the white beans and gets a tangy boost of flavor, richness, and moisture from the labneh. The flavors of fresh and dried herbs, savory Parmesan cheese, and bright black pepper make these burgers so craveable. These burgers are great between buns, as I've called for here, but they're also delicious served alongside my Cabbage, Cucumber & Sumac Slaw (page 111).

1 (15-ounce) **can white beans,** drained and rinsed

¼ **cup Labneh** (page 258)

1 **large shallot,** chopped

½ **cup** (packed) **fresh parsley,** chopped

1 **teaspoon dried oregano**

¼ **teaspoon salt**

½ **teaspoon black pepper**

1 **large egg**

1 **cup grated Parmesan cheese**

1 **cup panko breadcrumbs**

2 **tablespoons olive oil**

4 **burger buns,** for serving

1. Pat the white beans as dry as possible with a paper towel and add them to a food processor along with the labneh. Process, scraping down the sides as needed, until the mixture forms a coarse puree. Add the shallot, parsley, oregano, salt, and pepper. Pulse a few times so that everything is incorporated.

2. Beat the egg in a medium bowl. Add the white bean mixture, the Parmesan, and the breadcrumbs; mix until well combined. Divide the mixture into 4 portions, firmly patting them into disks about ½ inch thick. Set aside on a plate.

3. Heat the oil in a large nonstick skillet over medium heat. Add the burgers, ensuring they aren't crowding each other. Cook until golden brown, 4 to 5 minutes per side. Serve the burgers tucked into the buns with your favorite toppings.

White Zucchini Pizza with Garlicky Labneh

Serves 4 | Active Time: 20 minutes | Total Time: 45 minutes

How much do I love white pizza? That béchamel-meets-Alfredo sauce is so good, and for a lighter-yet-equally-delicious take, I use labneh thinned with olive oil and lemon. I definitely don't skimp on the garlic here, and neither should you. (I have even made a garlic-lovers version of this pizza for my husband, doubling the number of cloves!) This fun white pizza is an ideal blank canvas for tons of toppings, but I especially love it with a fresh, classic blend of zucchini, summer squash, and oregano.

1 pound store-bought pizza dough

1 small zucchini, thinly sliced

1 small summer squash, thinly sliced

¼ teaspoon salt

1¼ cups Labneh (page 258)

2 tablespoons extra-virgin olive oil

4 garlic cloves, minced

1 teaspoon dried oregano, divided

2 cups shredded low-moisture mozzarella cheese

¼ teaspoon crushed red pepper

1. Remove the pizza dough from the fridge; rest at room temperature while you prepare the veggies.

2. In a medium bowl, toss the zucchini and squash with the salt. Rest for 15 minutes. Set a strainer in a sink and add the veggies; using your hands, squeeze out as much water as possible. Return the veggies to the bowl and pat with paper towels to remove any excess moisture. Set aside.

3. Arrange a rack in the lower third of the oven and preheat to 450°F. Place a large parchment paper (round or rectangular) on a flat work surface.

4. Roll the pizza dough into the shape of the parchment and transfer them together to a pan.

5. In a small bowl, whisk the labneh, oil, garlic, and ½ teaspoon of the oregano. Spread the labneh mixture across the pizza. Top evenly with the mozzarella, the zucchini and squash, the remaining ½ teaspoon of oregano, and the crushed red pepper.

6. Bake until the crust is golden brown and the cheese is melted and bubbly, 15 to 18 minutes. Remove the pizza from the oven and let the pizza rest for 5 minutes before slicing and serving.

Stuffed Eggplant Parmesan

Serves 4   Active Time: 30 minutes   Total Time: 1 hour 10 minutes

What's better than eggplant Parmesan? Stuffed eggplant Parmesan! What I love about this meal is the hearty, tomato-y chickpeas hanging out between layers of eggplant and cheese. They're nourishing, satisfying, and rich in a way that complements everything else going on in this dish. I didn't know that my beloved eggplant parm was missing something until I tried this, but now I don't want to make it any other way.

3 tablespoons olive oil, plus more for coating

2 medium eggplants, halved lengthwise

1 small yellow onion, finely chopped

½ teaspoon salt, divided

½ teaspoon black pepper, divided

4 garlic cloves, minced

1 teaspoon zaatar

1½ cups prepared marinara sauce

1 (15-ounce) **can chickpeas,** drained and rinsed

½ cup chopped fresh basil

¾ cup shredded low-moisture mozzarella cheese

2 tablespoons grated Parmesan cheese

2 tablespoons panko breadcrumbs

1. Preheat the oven to 375°F. Coat a 9 × 13-inch baking dish with oil.

2. Using a spoon, carve the eggplant flesh from the halves into a medium bowl, leaving a border about ½ inch thick around the edges. Place the eggplant boats in the prepared baking dish. Roughly chop the eggplant flesh into pieces about ¼ inch thick and set aside.

3. Heat the oil in a large skillet over medium-high heat. Add the onion, ¼ teaspoon of the salt, and ¼ teaspoon of the pepper. Cook, stirring occasionally, until softened and browned, 5 to 7 minutes. Add the reserved chopped eggplant, the garlic, and zaatar. Cook, stirring occasionally, until the eggplant is browned and has released most of its moisture, 4 to 6 minutes. Add the marinara, chickpeas, basil, and the remaining ¼ teaspoon of salt and ¼ teaspoon of pepper. Cook for 5 minutes longer.

4. Divide the chickpea-eggplant stuffing between the 4 eggplant boats. Bake for 30 minutes. Remove the eggplant boats from the oven and top evenly with the mozzarella, Parmesan, and panko. Return the eggplant boats to the oven; continue baking until the cheese is melty and bubbly and the eggplant is tender, 15 to 20 minutes longer.

Spiced Couscous-Stuffed Peppers

Serves 4 | Active Time: 30 minutes | Total Time: 1 hour 10 minutes

While I enjoy a classic dish of peppers stuffed with Hashweh (page 217), there are plenty of other traditional options that don't use meat at all. A roasted stuffed vegetable is so central to regional Mediterranean cooking, and there's something deeply satisfying about making a delicious pilaf-style filling of couscous and lentils to tuck inside juicy bell peppers. To take things up a notch, I drizzle everything with my fresh Cucumber Yogurt Sauce (page 257). These spiced stuffed peppers are flavorful, filling little packages that will make any plant or meat eater happy.

Olive oil, for coating

½ cup brown lentils, rinsed and drained

½ cup fine couscous

½ teaspoon salt, divided

1 (7-ounce) **jar oil-packed julienned sun-dried tomatoes,** oil reserved

½ cup slivered almonds

½ cup crumbled feta cheese

4 green onions (whites and greens), chopped

2 garlic cloves, minced

1 teaspoon ground cumin

1 teaspoon dried thyme

½ teaspoon black pepper, divided

4 bell peppers, halved lengthwise and seeded

Cucumber Yogurt Sauce (page 257), for serving

1. Preheat the oven to 375°F. Coat a 9 × 13-inch baking dish with oil.

2. In a large saucepan, bring 1½ cups of water to a boil over high heat. Add the lentils and return to a boil. Reduce the heat to medium-low, cover the saucepan with a lid, and cook for 15 minutes.

3. Add the couscous and ¼ teaspoon of the salt to the lentils, cover the saucepan once more, and cook, allowing the couscous to absorb all of the remaining liquid and become plump, about 10 minutes. Remove the saucepan from the heat and rest, covered, for 5 minutes longer. Fluff the mixture with a fork.

4. Add the tomatoes and 2 tablespoons of the reserved tomato oil along with the almonds, feta, green onions, garlic, cumin, thyme, the remaining ¼ teaspoon of salt, and the pepper. Using the fork, stir to combine.

5. Arrange the bell peppers cut side up in the prepared baking dish. It's okay if they look crowded—the peppers will shrink as they roast. Divide the lentil-couscous stuffing between the 8 bell-pepper boats.

6. Cover the baking dish tightly with aluminum foil and bake for 30 minutes. Remove the foil and continue to bake the peppers, uncovered, until tender, 10 to 15 minutes longer. Drizzle with the Cucumber Yogurt Sauce (if using).

6

Seafood Mains

Skillet Cilantro-Lime Salmon

Serves 4 | Active Time: 25 minutes | Total Time: 25 minutes

My dad is notorious for finishing seafood dishes with cilantro, butter, and garlic. He does this with salmon, shrimp, cod, and even lobster. Everyone always asks, What's that sauce?! *I think you'll love it, too. Bright green, fresh, herby, citrusy, easy—this deceptively simple dish is all of my favorite things in one meal. I like pairing salmon with this zesty sauce, but you can use any firm-fleshed fish you like.*

4 (6-ounce) **skin-on salmon fillets**

½ teaspoon salt

½ teaspoon black pepper

½ teaspoon dried mint

2 tablespoons olive oil

1 tablespoon salted butter

½ cup fresh cilantro, chopped

4 garlic cloves, grated

Zest and juice of 1 lime

1. Pat the salmon dry with paper towels. Season with the salt, pepper, and mint.

2. Heat the oil in a large nonstick skillet over medium-high heat. Place the salmon skin side up in the skillet. Sear, undisturbed, until the salmon is opaque three-quarters of the way through and releases easily from the pan with a spatula, 4 to 6 minutes. Carefully flip the salmon; sear until the fish is just cooked through and flakes easily with a fork, 1 to 2 minutes longer. Transfer the fillets to a serving platter.

3. Add the butter, cilantro, garlic, lime zest, and lime juice to the skillet. Swirl the pan around to evenly distribute the butter. Spoon the cilantro-lime butter sauce over the salmon and serve immediately.

Balsamic-Roasted Salmon

Serves 4 | Active Time: 15 minutes | Total Time: 30 minutes

You can't go wrong with the Mediterranean flavors of basil and balsamic. These ingredients are familiar in salads and sandwiches, but I think salmon is the big sleeper hit. It's rich, steaky, and stands up perfectly to these fresh, assertive tastes. Even better, this recipe is a one-baking-dish kind of meal because everything is marinated, roasted, and served in the same baking dish.

3 tablespoons balsamic glaze

2 tablespoons olive oil

1 teaspoon dried oregano

½ teaspoon garlic powder

½ teaspoon salt

½ teaspoon black pepper

4 (6-ounce) **skin-on salmon fillets**

1 cup grape tomatoes, halved

¼ cup fresh basil leaves, chopped

1. Preheat the oven to 400°F.

2. In a 9 × 13-inch baking dish, whisk the balsamic, oil, oregano, garlic powder, salt, and pepper. Add the salmon; gently toss in the marinade until fully coated.

3. Place the salmon skin side down in the baking dish. Scatter the tomatoes around the fish, and toss them in any excess marinade.

4. Roast until the salmon is opaque and flaky, 15 to 18 minutes. Scatter the basil over the top.

Grilled Salmon & Veggie Kabobs

Makes 8 skewers | Active Time: 30 minutes | Total Time: 30 minutes

I just think everything is more fun to eat on a stick! This is a little trick I use to get my kids to try new things, and it's especially useful in guiding them to eat their veggies. To make these kabobs even more appealing, I use a rainbow of colors: green peppers, red onions, pink salmon, and bright yellow lemons. How pretty is that? (Those thinly sliced, slightly charred lemons are so good by the way—they're not just a garnish!) And don't worry if you don't have a grill because you can just as easily cook these kabobs stovetop on a grill pan or in a nonstick skillet. Pro tip: Try sliding the cooked kabobs into an Arabic-style pita with a swipe of Toum (page 261).

2 pounds skinless salmon fillets, cut into 2-inch cubes

4 small lemons, 1 juiced and 3 very thinly sliced

1 large green bell pepper, seeded and cut into 1-inch cubes

1 large red onion, cut into 1-inch cubes

3 tablespoons olive oil

2 garlic cloves, grated

1 teaspoon dried oregano

½ teaspoon ground cumin

½ teaspoon salt

½ teaspoon black pepper

1. Set up your work station with a large baking sheet and eight metal or wooden skewers. If you're using wooden skewers and you're grilling outside, soak them in cold water for at least 30 minutes before cooking. Heat a grill to medium-high heat.

2. Gently pat the salmon as dry as possible with paper towels. Thread a piece of salmon, a folded slice of lemon, a cube of bell pepper, and a cube of onion on one skewer, ensuring that there is about ¼ inch of space between each ingredient. Continue threading the ingredients, alternating each time, until you are about 1 inch from the end of the skewer. Set the finished skewer on the baking sheet. Repeat with the remaining skewers and ingredients.

3. In a small bowl, whisk the lemon juice, oil, garlic, oregano, cumin, salt, and black pepper. Brush the skewers with the dressing, using all of it.

4. Grill the skewers until the salmon is opaque and cooked through and the veggies are tender, 3 to 4 minutes per side. Transfer the skewers to a large platter and enjoy.

Cod with Browned Butter–Sumac Breadcrumbs

Serves 4   Active Time: 15 minutes   Total Time: 25 minutes

I love crispy, breaded fish. (See page 187 for my Cashew-Crusted Cod & Green Beans!) Sometimes, though, instead of going for the traditional route with dredging stations, I like to build on that toasty, crunchy coating by dressing up simple breadcrumbs in a skillet. This dish reminds me of the Midwest, a region that really knows how to use a breadcrumb. I've seen them made from buttery crackers, cheesy crackers, cornflakes, potato chips . . . I could go on! Here, I'm nodding to both the Midwest and the Middle East with breadcrumbs flavored with nutty browned butter and bright, tart sumac. Does it get any better than that?

4 (6-ounce) **cod fillets**

2 teaspoons **dried thyme**

½ teaspoon **salt**

½ teaspoon **black pepper**

3 tablespoons **salted butter,** divided

½ cup **panko breadcrumbs**

2 teaspoons **ground sumac**

1. Pat the cod fillets dry with a paper towel. Sprinkle with the thyme, salt, and pepper. Set aside.

2. Melt 2 tablespoons of the butter in a large nonstick skillet over medium heat. Cook, swirling the pan, until the butter begins browning, 2 to 3 minutes. (Don't leave the skillet—this happens faster than you think!) Stir in the panko and sumac. Toast, stirring constantly, until browned and fragrant, 1 to 2 minutes longer. Transfer the breadcrumbs to a small bowl and set aside.

3. Wipe out the skillet and heat the remaining 1 tablespoon butter over medium heat. Add the cod fillets, making sure they're not crowding one another. Sear, undisturbed, until the cod is opaque three-quarters of the way through and releases easily from the pan with a spatula, 6 to 8 minutes. Carefully flip the cod; sear until the fish is just cooked through and flakes easily with a fork, 2 to 3 minutes longer.

4. Transfer the fillets to a serving platter. Scatter the reserved browned butter–sumac breadcrumbs on top and serve.

Cashew-Crusted Cod & Green Beans

Serves 4 | Active Time: 15 minutes | Total Time: 30 minutes

This is one of those meals that looks impressive because of the crunchy cashew-crumb crust on the cod, but it comes together pretty quickly on one baking sheet. The yogurt-and-mustard mixture helps the spiced-crumb coating stick to the cod and lock in the fish's delicate flavor. Sometimes I'll substitute the crisp-tender green beans here for trimmed asparagus in the summer or thinly sliced broccoli in the winter, so feel free to do so, too.

4 (6-ounce) **cod fillets**

¾ teaspoon **salt,** divided

½ teaspoon **black pepper,** divided

¼ cup **Greek yogurt**

2 tablespoons **Dijon mustard**

1 cup **cashews,** finely chopped or pulsed in a food processor

½ cup **panko breadcrumbs**

1 teaspoon **paprika**

1 teaspoon **ground cumin**

1 teaspoon **garlic powder**

Olive oil cooking spray

1 pound **green beans,** trimmed

1. Preheat the oven to 425°F. Line a large baking sheet with parchment paper.

2. Pat the cod dry with paper towels and season with ½ teaspoon of the salt and ¼ teaspoon of the pepper. Set aside.

3. In a large bowl, whisk the yogurt and mustard. Add the cod fillets, turning each one with your hands until evenly coated. Set aside.

4. In a medium bowl, combine the cashews, breadcrumbs, paprika, cumin, and garlic powder. Working with one fillet at a time, evenly coat the cod on both sides in the cashew mixture, gently pressing on the fish to help the cashew crumbs adhere. Place each crumb-coated fillet on the prepared baking sheet and generously coat with the cooking spray.

5. Scatter the green beans around the fish, spray with the cooking spray, and season with the remaining ½ teaspoon of salt and ¼ teaspoon of pepper. Roast until the cashew crumbs are golden brown and the cod flakes easily with a fork, 15 to 18 minutes.

Sizzling Shrimp Scampi with Tomatoes

Serves 4 | Active Time: 20 minutes | Total Time: 20 minutes

The first time I cooked this dish, I was craving classic Mediterranean shrimp scampi and wanted to give it a twist. So, I added some sizzling heat and color from paprika, crushed red pepper, and bursting cherry tomatoes. I played up the rich, traditional notes of butter and garlic and used vegetable broth to make a cozy sauce right in the skillet. Last but not least, I hit the shrimp with a dash of red wine vinegar right when it finished cooking to brighten up all the flavors. This recipe is now the only way I want to eat shrimp scampi. Do I recommend serving it with some crusty bread for dipping? Of course I do!

1 pound large shrimp, peeled and deveined

½ teaspoon paprika

¼ teaspoon salt

¼ teaspoon black pepper

2 tablespoons (¼ stick) **salted butter**

2 tablespoons olive oil

4 garlic cloves, minced

½ teaspoon crushed red pepper, or to taste

1 pint cherry tomatoes

¼ cup vegetable broth

1 tablespoon red wine vinegar

Chopped fresh parsley, for serving

1. Pat the shrimp dry with paper towels. Season all over with the paprika, salt, and black pepper. Set aside.

2. Melt the butter and oil in a large skillet over medium-high heat. Add the garlic and crushed red pepper. Cook, stirring constantly, until fragrant, about 30 seconds. Add the tomatoes and broth. Cook, stirring occasionally, until the tomatoes begin to soften and burst, 6 to 8 minutes.

3. Add the shrimp to the skillet. Cook, basting the shrimp with the sauce and stirring occasionally, until the shrimp are tender and opaque throughout, 3 to 5 minutes. Remove the skillet from the heat. Drizzle with the vinegar and sprinkle with the parsley. Serve immediately.

Crispy Rice & Shrimp

Serves 6 | Active Time: 30 minutes | Total Time: 1 hour

I grew up enjoying the fluffiest rice and pilaf dishes with many meals, but I remember when my mom accidentally cooked a pot of rice on high heat. The golden-brown crust at the bottom of the pot was so good that I jokingly asked my mom to do it again. It was only later that we both learned about tahdig, a Persian method of cooking crispy-edged rice. It's a technique that's so genius and delicious, I knew I had to learn to make it myself. When I want to turn this crispy rice into a full meal, I'll steam shrimp on top of the rice before flipping the whole thing crispy side up. Let me tell you, the first time you make perfect crispy rice is one of the greatest feelings. So, take a deep breath before flipping and trust!

1½ cups basmati rice, rinsed until the water runs clear

3 tablespoons Greek yogurt

1 large egg

2 teaspoons ground turmeric

3 tablespoons salted butter

1 pound large shrimp, peeled and deveined

2 tablespoons chopped fresh dill, plus more for serving

1 tablespoon olive oil

1 teaspoon ground sumac

¼ teaspoon salt

1. Bring a small pot of salted water to a boil over high heat. Add the rice and cook, stirring occasionally, until al dente, about 5 minutes. Drain the rice and rinse with cold water.

2. In a large bowl, mix the yogurt, egg, and turmeric. Add the cooked rice and stir to combine.

3. Melt the butter in a 10-inch nonstick or cast-iron skillet over medium-high heat. Add the yogurt-rice mixture, gently pressing it into the bottom and up the sides of the skillet. Allow to cook, undisturbed, for 5 minutes. Reduce the heat to medium-low. Cover the skillet with a fitted lid wrapped in a clean kitchen towel (the towel absorbs excess moisture). Cook until the rice at the edge of the skillet is golden brown, about 15 minutes.

4. Meanwhile, in a large bowl, toss the shrimp with the dill, oil, sumac, and salt.

5. Uncover the skillet. Arrange the shrimp on top of the rice and cover the skillet once more. Cook the shrimp for 5 minutes. Remove the lid and, using tongs, flip the shrimp. Replace the lid and continue cooking until the shrimp are pink and opaque, about 5 minutes longer. Remove the skillet from the heat. Let it sit, uncovered, for 5 minutes.

6. Gently run a spatula along the edges of the skillet to loosen the crust. Top the skillet with a serving platter that's larger in circumference. Carefully yet swiftly flip the skillet. (You've got this!) Top with the dill and serve immediately.

Harissa-Grilled Shrimp Skewers

Makes 4 skewers | Active Time: 15 minutes | Total Time: 25 minutes

Harissa is a spicy, smoky, richly flavored chili pepper paste common in Middle Eastern and North African cooking. It's usually made from wonderful things like dry red chiles, garlic, fresh citrus, spices, and olive oil. But every batch of harissa is different depending on the chiles used, the strength of the garlic, where the olive oil is from, regional traditions, or individual tweaks. Harissa is a magical ingredient that boosts everything it comes in contact with, especially thick, juicy shrimp. Here, I'm using harissa as a marinade with fresh citrus and seven spice, which really holds up to the smoky char of the grill. But if you're not a griller—or if it's January and you live in Michigan, like me—feel free to cook these shrimp inside on a grill pan or in a large nonstick skillet.

¼ **cup harissa paste**

1 **tablespoon olive oil**

Zest and juice of 1 lemon

2 **garlic cloves,** minced

1 **teaspoon Seven Spice** (page 259 or store-bought)

¼ **teaspoon salt**

20 **large shrimp** (about 1 pound), peeled and deveined

1. Set up your work station with a large plate and four metal or wooden skewers. If you're using wooden skewers and you're grilling outside, soak them in cold water for at least 30 minutes before cooking. Heat a grill to medium-high heat.

2. In a large bowl, whisk the harissa, oil, lemon zest, lemon juice, garlic, seven spice, and salt. Add the shrimp and toss to coat. Let sit for 15 minutes.

3. Divide the marinated shrimp between the four skewers, ensuring that there is about ¼ inch of space between each piece. Set the finished skewers on the plate.

4. Grill the skewers until the shrimp is firm and opaque, about 2 minutes per side. Transfer the skewers to a serving platter and enjoy.

Mahi-mahi with Zaatar & Roasted Lemons

Serves 4 | Active Time: 10 minutes | Total Time: 25 minutes

When you close your eyes and picture the Mediterranean, I'm pretty sure lemons and olives come to mind. This is one dish I go to again and again when I want the smells and flavors of the Mediterranean coast to hit my plate, because whether it's summer or winter you can find lemons and olives in any store. Roasting lemons cut side down while the fish cooks is such an easy way to build deep flavor, and the crushed olives get extra plump in those amazing juices. This is a one-pan dinner that cooks your protein and your sauce at the same time, meaning it's a meal I would make any weekday—but it's really nice for a dinner party, too!

4 (6-ounce) **mahi-mahi fillets**

2 tablespoons extra-virgin olive oil

1 tablespoon zaatar

½ teaspoon salt

½ teaspoon black pepper

1 cup whole green olives

2 lemons, halved

1. Preheat the oven to 425°F.

2. Place the fillets in a 9 × 13-inch baking dish. Drizzle with the oil and season with the zaatar, salt, and pepper.

3. Using the flat side of your knife, crush the olives to loosen and remove the pits. Scatter the olives around the fish. Nestle the lemons cut side down in the baking dish.

4. Roast the mahi-mahi until it's opaque throughout and flakes easily with a fork, 12 to 14 minutes. Remove the baking dish from the oven. Using tongs, pick up the lemon halves and squeeze them liberally over the fish. Serve immediately.

Lemon-Dill Tuna Patties

Makes 4 patties | Active Time: 20 minutes | Total Time: 20 minutes

Easy, affordable, and flavorful, these tuna patties were the weeknight pantry inspiration of one hungry and busy mom (me!). Canned tuna, breadcrumbs, and kitchen staples like Greek yogurt and mustard come together so quickly for a satisfying meal that's greater than the sum of its parts. And the fresh dill and lemon honestly make this humble recipe sneakily fabulous. These patties are just as great alongside a crunchy salad as they are served with my Cucumber Yogurt Sauce (page 257).

2 (5-ounce) **cans albacore tuna in water,** drained

1 large egg

Zest of 1 small lemon

3 tablespoons Greek yogurt

2 tablespoons chopped fresh dill

1 tablespoon Dijon mustard

¼ teaspoon salt

¼ teaspoon black pepper

½ cup panko breadcrumbs

2 tablespoons olive oil

Cucumber Yogurt Sauce (page 257), for serving

1. In a medium bowl, using a fork, stir the tuna, egg, lemon zest, yogurt, dill, mustard, salt, and pepper until thoroughly combined. Add the breadcrumbs and stir again until well combined. Using your hands, divide and firmly shape the mixture into 4 patties.

2. Heat the oil in a large nonstick skillet over medium-high heat. Add the patties, being careful not to crowd them, and cook until golden brown, 3 to 4 minutes per side. Serve with Cucumber Yogurt Sauce.

7

Chicken & Beef Mains

Yogurt & Rosemary Roasted Chicken Thighs

Serves 4 | Active Time: 10 minutes | Total Time: 40 minutes (plus marinating)

If you've never marinated chicken in yogurt before, you're in for a treat! This is a trick my mom taught me for keeping chicken super juicy, no matter the cooking method. I've tried this yogurt marinade on chicken that's grilled, air-fried, sautéed, and roasted—you really can't go wrong. A quick rest in the marinade is all you need for delicious browning, juicy meat, and plenty of flavor in this recipe, but if you have the time, let the chicken marinate for up to twenty-four hours for peak juiciness.

½ **cup Greek yogurt**

6 **garlic cloves,** minced

1 **tablespoon Dijon mustard**

2 **tablespoons fresh rosemary leaves,** chopped

2 **teaspoons dried oregano**

2 **teaspoons paprika**

½ **teaspoon salt**

½ **teaspoon black pepper**

3 **pounds bone-in skin-on chicken thighs** (about 8 large)

1. In a large bowl, mix the yogurt, garlic, mustard, rosemary, oregano, paprika, salt, and pepper. Set aside.

2. Pat the chicken thighs dry with paper towels and transfer them to the bowl with the yogurt marinade. Toss the chicken until well coated, then cover the bowl and transfer to the fridge. Let the chicken marinate for at least 30 minutes or up to 24 hours.

3. When you're ready to roast the chicken, preheat the oven to 425°F. Line a large baking sheet with parchment paper.

4. Arrange the chicken thighs on the prepared baking sheet. Roast until the chicken skin is browned and the internal temperature is 165°F, about 30 minutes.

Seven Spice Roast Chicken & Pomegranate Potatoes

Serves 4 | Active Time: 15 minutes | Total Time: 1 hour 30 minutes

Pomegranate molasses is most often used to make the bright, tart dressing for classic fattoush salad (see page 101). It has a sweet-sour flavor that is iconic in Mediterranean cooking, and just a dash can really transform the flavor of a dish. There's a reason it's one of my eight Mediterranean staples (see page 16). The second most popular way to cook with pomegranate molasses is to whisk it into marinades and sauces—it gets so caramelized, savory, and sticky in the oven, making everything it touches quite literally finger-licking good. This got me thinking: how great would it be to toss potatoes in a pomegranate-molasses-spiked sauce and then roast them until fabulously browned in chicken drippings? Um . . . so good! This whole-roasted, crispy-skinned chicken gets a deep boost of flavor from seven spice (another one of my Mediterranean staples), making this simple, unfussy, but seriously special dish a perfect mash-up of some of my favorite flavors.

1 whole chicken (about 3½ pounds)

1 tablespoon Seven Spice (page 259 or store-bought)

1½ teaspoons salt, divided

1½ teaspoons black pepper, divided

1 small yellow onion, quartered

8 sprigs of fresh thyme

1 orange, halved

2 tablespoons pomegranate molasses

2 tablespoons olive oil

1 pound baby potatoes, halved

1. Preheat the oven to 375°F.

2. Remove the giblets from the cavity of the chicken and, using paper towels, pat the chicken as dry as possible. Place the chicken in a 9 × 13-inch baking dish and generously season all over with the seven spice, 1 teaspoon of the salt, and 1 teaspoon of the pepper. Turn the chicken breast side up. Loosely stuff the onion and thyme into the cavity. Nestle the orange halves cut side down beside the chicken. Set aside.

3. In a medium bowl, whisk the pomegranate molasses, oil, and the remaining ½ teaspoon of salt and ½ teaspoon of pepper. Add the potatoes and toss to coat. Arrange the potatoes around the chicken and orange halves.

4. Roast, rotating the baking dish once halfway through, until the potatoes are tender and the chicken is golden brown and cooked through (a thermometer inserted into the thigh should read 165°F), 60 to 75 minutes. Using tongs, squeeze the orange halves over the potatoes. Let the chicken rest for 20 minutes before carving and serving.

Lemony Grilled Chicken Kabobs

Makes 8 skewers | Active Time: 15 minutes | Total Time: 30 minutes (plus marinating)

We grill more kabobs than burgers in my family, and this chicken kabob recipe is one we enjoy all year round. In the winter, when our grill is buried under a tundra of fresh snowfall, we'll roast these kabobs in a four-hundred-degree oven, turning them once, until browned and cooked through (twenty-five to thirty minutes). It's like time travel in the dark months of February: that fresh lemon flavor takes us right back to warm summer days on the patio. For this recipe, though, let's pretend it's late June, the kids are out of school, and we're eating smoke-kissed kabobs outside. So good!

Zest and juice of 2 lemons

2 tablespoons olive oil

4 garlic cloves, grated

2 teaspoons paprika

2 teaspoons ground turmeric

1 teaspoon ground cumin

1 teaspoon salt

1 teaspoon black pepper

2½ pounds boneless, skinless chicken breasts (about 4), cut into 1½-inch cubes

1. In a large bowl, whisk the lemon zest, lemon juice, oil, garlic, paprika, turmeric, cumin, salt, and pepper. Add the chicken and toss to combine. Cover and marinate in the fridge for 30 minutes.

2. Meanwhile, set up your work station with a baking sheet and eight metal or wooden skewers. If you're using wooden skewers and you're grilling outside, soak them in cold water for at least 30 minutes before cooking. Heat a grill to medium-high heat.

3. Thread the chicken pieces onto one skewer, leaving about 1 inch at the bottom and top of the skewer and ensuring that there is ¼ inch of space between each piece. Set the finished skewer on the baking sheet. Repeat with the remaining chicken and skewers.

4. Grill the chicken kabobs, turning every 5 minutes, until they're cooked through and golden brown, 10 to 15 minutes total. Transfer the skewers to a serving platter and serve.

Chicken & Zucchini Skillet

Serves 4   Active Time: 30 minutes   Total Time: 40 minutes

This is a great one-skillet meal that you can endlessly customize with vegetables and spices. Silky zucchini, briny capers, and salty Parmesan cheese is my current go-to—but feel free to swap in broccoli or bell peppers for the zucchini, or, if you crave heat, sub pickled pepperoncini and a teaspoon of chili flakes for the capers and oregano. We love eating this dish over rice, tossed with cooked pasta, or all on its own.

1½ pounds boneless, skinless chicken breasts, cut into 1-inch pieces

2 teaspoons dried oregano

1 teaspoon onion powder

½ teaspoon salt, divided

½ teaspoon black pepper, divided

2 tablespoons (¼ stick) **salted butter,** divided

1 small yellow onion, diced

¼ cup capers, with their brine

2 garlic cloves, minced

2 medium zucchinis (about 1 pound), halved and thinly sliced

¼ cup grated Parmesan cheese

1. In a large bowl, season the chicken with the oregano, onion powder, ¼ teaspoon of the salt, and ¼ teaspoon of the pepper. Set aside.

2. Melt 1 tablespoon of the butter in a large nonstick skillet over medium-high heat. Add the chicken in a single layer and cook, undisturbed, until lightly browned on one side, about 3 minutes. Stir the chicken and continue cooking, stirring occasionally, until the chicken is cooked through and lightly browned all over, 7 to 10 minutes longer. Transfer to a plate and set aside.

3. Heat the remaining 1 tablespoon of butter in the same skillet over medium-high heat. Add the onion, capers with their brine, and garlic. Cook, stirring frequently and scraping up any browned bits from the bottom of the pan, until the onion has softened and the caper brine has evaporated, about 5 minutes.

4. Add the zucchini and the remaining ¼ teaspoon of salt and ¼ teaspoon of pepper. Cook, stirring occasionally, until softened and browned, 5 to 7 minutes.

5. Remove the skillet from the heat and stir in the reserved chicken. Sprinkle everything with the Parmesan.

Cast-Iron Sumac Chicken

Serves 4 | Active Time: 15 minutes | Total Time: 45 minutes

As you're well aware if you've been cooking your way through this book, tart-sweet sumac is one of my favorite flavors in savory cooking (and one of my eight Mediterranean staples; see page 16). And if you're thinking that cinnamon should be saved for the dessert chapter, think again! The warm, earthy flavor complements bright sumac and pungent garlic perfectly. This is an ideal one-skillet meal for cozy, colder months—I honestly think the smell that perfumes your kitchen when you cook this chicken should be bottled and sold as a scented candle.

8 skin-on chicken drumsticks

2 teaspoons ground sumac

1 teaspoon garlic powder

¾ teaspoon salt

½ teaspoon black pepper

½ teaspoon ground cinnamon

2 tablespoons olive oil

1 red onion, sliced into wedges

1. Preheat the oven to 425°F.

2. Pat the chicken dry with paper towels. Season with the sumac, garlic powder, salt, pepper, and cinnamon.

3. Heat the oil in a cast-iron skillet over medium heat. Add the chicken fleshy side down. Cook, undisturbed, until the skin is browned and crisp, about 5 minutes. Using tongs, flip the chicken. Cook for 3 minutes longer.

4. Remove the skillet from the heat. Arrange the onion between the drumsticks (it's okay if the skillet looks crowded—everything will shrink during roasting). Transfer the skillet to the oven and roast until the chicken is cooked to an internal temperature of 165°F, 25 to 30 minutes. Carefully remove the skillet from the oven and rest for 5 minutes before serving.

My Favorite Chicken Shawarma

Serves 4 | Active Time: 25 minutes | Total Time: 25 minutes

True chicken shawarma—one that's made on a spit and shaved into perfectly charred, seasoned pieces—is hard to emulate at home. But after much trial and error, I can confidently say I've nailed down the spice mix for a recipe that tastes just like my favorite place to eat chicken shawarma when I was growing up. This easy, made-for-home method only requires a heavy-bottomed skillet to cook the marinated chicken, so it gets browned without burning. If you have the time, definitely let the chicken marinate for maximum flavor. If you don't, this recipe still makes incredibly delicious chicken shawarma, which you can enjoy on its own, in salads, or wrapped in warm pita with garlicky toum and pickled turnips.

1½ pounds boneless, skinless chicken thighs, thinly sliced

3 tablespoons olive oil

2 tablespoons lemon juice

4 garlic cloves, minced

1 teaspoon paprika

¾ teaspoon salt

½ teaspoon ground cardamom

½ teaspoon ground cumin

¼ teaspoon ground cinnamon

¼ teaspoon crushed red pepper

Toum, for serving (optional; page 261)

Arabic-style pita, for serving (optional)

1. Pat the chicken dry with paper towels. In a large bowl, whisk the oil, lemon juice, garlic, paprika, salt, cardamom, cumin, cinnamon, and crushed red pepper. Add the chicken and gently toss to coat. (If you'd like to marinate the chicken, cover the bowl and rest in the fridge for up to 24 hours.)

2. Heat a large heavy-bottomed skillet over medium-high heat. Add the chicken and cook, stirring occasionally, until the chicken is browned and cooked through, 12 to 15 minutes. Transfer the chicken shawarma to a serving platter and enjoy with the Toum and pita (if using).

Mama's Beef Shawarma

Serves 8 | Active Time: 20 minutes | Total Time: 30 minutes (plus marinating)

Shawarma is an iconic Lebanese street food. Traditionally it's made by stacking large pieces of marinated steak on a vertical spit, cooking everything over a live-fire grill, and very thinly shaving the smoky, spiced, ridiculously good meat to order. For a quicker way to make it at home, my mom requests thinly sliced flank steak from the butcher, which she marinates and cooks herself on the stovetop. Listen, the longer you marinate the steak, the better, so if you can prep your steak up to twenty-four hours ahead, do so! I usually only have the patience for one hour, though, and the flavor is still truly amazing. My mom spent years trying to perfect this marinade to make it replicable to our favorite street food, and, let me tell you, it's the closest I've ever tasted!

2 pounds flank steak

¼ cup olive oil

¼ cup white vinegar

Zest and juice of 1 lemon

4 garlic cloves, minced

1 teaspoon salt

1 teaspoon ground allspice

1 teaspoon ground cumin

½ teaspoon ground cloves

½ teaspoon ground cardamom

½ teaspoon ground cinnamon

½ teaspoon dried oregano

½ teaspoon paprika

1 small yellow onion, thinly sliced

3 bay leaves

Tahini Sauce, for serving (optional; page 256)

Arabic-style pita, for serving (optional)

1. Very thinly slice the flank steak into strips about ¼ inch thick. Set aside.

2. In a large bowl, whisk the oil, vinegar, lemon zest, lemon juice, garlic, salt, allspice, cumin, cloves, cardamom, cinnamon, oregano, and paprika until well combined. Add the steak, onion, and bay leaves; toss to fully coat in the marinade. Cover and marinate in the fridge for 1 hour or up to 24 hours.

3. Heat a large heavy-bottomed skillet over medium-high heat. Add the steak mixture along with any leftover marinade. Cook, stirring occasionally, until the steak is cooked through and the onion is tender, 8 to 10 minutes. Using tongs, transfer the steak and onion to a large serving bowl.

4. Bring the remaining cooking juices to a boil over high heat. Cook, stirring occasionally, until thickened and reduced by half, 3 to 5 minutes. Pour the reduction over the beef shawarma and serve hot with the Tahini Sauce and pita (if using).

Tahini Kafta

Serves 8   Active Time: 20 minutes   Total Time: 50 minutes

Kafta is like the meatball of the Middle East. It's usually ground beef or lamb mixed with spices, herbs, and onions, then hand-formed into an oblong shape or meatballs. My mom made kafta two ways growing up: grilled or in a tomato stew with potatoes and vegetables. I learned this tahini kafta recipe from a Jordanian friend and loved it from first bite. It's usually made with fried potatoes, which get smothered in the tahini sauce and then baked alongside the kafta, but I usually like to nix the potatoes and double the number of kafta I can fit in the pan (kafta goes fast in my house!). This recipe is so good I instantly started making it for my family on the regular, and I think it'll be in your weekly rotations, too. Pro tip: Saucy tahini kafta pairs perfectly with Vermicelli Rice (page 224).

Olive oil cooking spray

2 pounds 85% lean ground beef

1 cup minced yellow onion

½ cup chopped fresh parsley, plus more for serving

3 teaspoons Seven Spice (page 259 or store-bought)

2 teaspoons ground cumin

1 teaspoon ground cinnamon

1 teaspoon ground coriander

1 teaspoon salt

½ teaspoon black pepper

1 cup Tahini Sauce (page 256)

Vermicelli Rice, for serving (optional; page 224)

1. Preheat the oven to 400°F. Coat a large baking dish with the cooking spray.

2. In a large bowl, gently mix the beef, onion, parsley, seven spice, cumin, cinnamon, coriander, salt, and pepper until well combined. Scoop ¼ cup of the mixture into your hands, and roll it into a meatball. Place the finished meatball in the prepared baking dish. Repeat with the remaining meatballs.

3. Bake the kafta until browned and just cooked through, about 20 minutes. Flip each kafta and pour the Tahini Sauce on top, turning the kafta until they're coated in the sauce. Return the kafta to the oven. Continue baking until the tahini has thickened and darkened slightly, about 10 minutes longer. Sprinkle with more parsley and serve over the Vermicelli Rice (if using).

Hashweh

Serves 4 | Active Time: 25 minutes | Total Time: 25 minutes

The word hashweh *in Arabic translates to "stuffing." This spiced ground beef dish is a quintessential recipe that we use for stuffing grape leaves, eggplant, peppers, squash, and so much more. (Mediterranean cooking loves a stuffed vegetable!) Sometimes, hashweh is mixed with rice for a heartier filling or used as a condiment itself to build satisfaction and flavor. It's commonly seen spooned over Vermicelli Rice (page 224), a fresh batch of Baba's Classic Hummus (page 66), or creamy Spaghetti with Garlicky Yogurt Sauce (page 163). It's such a tasty and versatile recipe that my family and I also enjoy hashweh on its own with some pita bread for scooping. I sometimes even like to add a little ketchup on the side when I enjoy it with pita—yum!*

3 tablespoons olive oil

2 large yellow onions, diced

1 teaspoon salt, divided

1 pound ground beef

¼ cup toasted pine nuts, plus more for serving

1 tablespoon Seven Spice (page 259 or store-bought)

½ teaspoon ground sumac

Chopped fresh parsley, for serving

1. Heat the oil in a medium skillet over medium heat. Add the onions and ½ teaspoon of the salt. Cook until soft, about 10 minutes.

2. Add the beef and cook, stirring often, until tender and browned, about 10 minutes longer. Stir in the pine nuts, seven spice, sumac, and remaining ½ teaspoon of salt.

3. Sprinkle the hashweh with the parsley and serve.

Steak in Garlicky Tomato Sauce

Serves 4 | Active Time: 25 minutes | Total Time: 25 minutes

I grew up thinking this steak was a classic Lebanese recipe—it was on rotation so often at our house alongside all my other favorite Lebanese dishes. When I asked my mom about its origin, though, she said it was just something she learned from her mom, and something my grandma learned from hers. None of my Lebanese friends had ever heard of it! Well, however it came about, it's a genius way to cook steak. This dish is made in one skillet with a few super flavorful ingredients, so each one does its part to shine. It's hearty and a little saucy (goals!), and I often serve it alongside my Tomato Rice Pilaf (page 226) or Sumac Sweet Potato Wedges (page 229).

4 New York strip steaks, about 1 inch thick

1 teaspoon salt

1 teaspoon black pepper

1 tablespoon olive oil

1 small yellow onion, halved and thinly sliced

2 garlic cloves, minced

1 teaspoon Seven Spice (page 259 or store-bought)

1 teaspoon dried thyme

¼ cup tomato paste

1. Pat the steaks dry with a paper towel. Season all over with the salt and pepper.

2. Heat the oil in a large nonstick skillet over medium-high heat. Add the steaks, making sure they're not touching each other, and cook to your desired doneness, 3 to 4 minutes per side for medium-rare. Transfer the steaks to a plate.

3. Reduce the heat to medium and add the onion to the skillet. Cook, stirring occasionally, until softened and browned, about 5 minutes. Add the garlic, seven spice, and thyme. Cook, stirring constantly, until very fragrant, about 30 seconds longer.

4. Add the tomato paste and ¾ cup of water. Bring to a simmer, stirring and scraping up any browned bits from the bottom of the pan. Continue simmering until the sauce has thickened, 2 to 3 minutes.

5. Reduce the heat to medium-low. Return the steaks and any resting juices to the skillet. Spoon the sauce and onion over the steaks until they're coated and just warmed through, about 1 minute, and serve immediately.

Mediterranean-Style BBQ Flank Steak

Serves 4 | Active Time: 15 minutes | Total Time: 20 minutes

Do you love a sweet, tangy, smoky glaze on your grilled steak? For those of you nodding, you need to try this Mediterranean spin on classic barbecue sauce made naturally tangy-sweet with pomegranate molasses. Pomegranate molasses is one of those MVP ingredients that can be delicate, floral, rich, and pungent all at once. It lends itself so well to cooking methods like grilling, where it gets caramelized and slightly smoky. Try this recipe in the summer alongside Pomegranate Green Bean Salad (page 123) and thank me later!

2 pounds flank steak, about 1 inch thick

1½ teaspoons salt

1 teaspoon black pepper

2 tablespoons olive oil

2 tablespoons pomegranate molasses

1 tablespoon honey

1 tablespoon red wine vinegar

1 teaspoon garlic powder

1 teaspoon ground cumin

1 teaspoon ground coriander

1. Preheat the grill to medium-high heat. Pat the steak dry with paper towels and season with the salt and pepper.

2. In a small bowl, whisk the oil, pomegranate molasses, honey, vinegar, garlic powder, cumin, and coriander. Brush half of the marinade all over the steak.

3. Grill the steak, flipping and brushing it with the remaining marinade every 2 minutes, until it reaches your desired doneness, about 4 minutes per side for medium-rare. Transfer the steak to a cutting board and rest for 5 minutes.

4. Thinly slice the steak against the grain. Serve warm, drizzled with any remaining resting juices.

8

Sides

Vermicelli Rice

Serves 8 | Active Time: 10 minutes | Total Time: 30 minutes

I cook vermicelli rice at least twice a month and could probably make it with my eyes closed if the hot stove wasn't a hazard. It's an essential recipe that pairs well with everything, from Tahini Kafta (page 214) to Hashweh (page 217) to Lemony Grilled Chicken Kabobs (page 205). Traditionally, it's most often enjoyed with a wide array of tomato-based stews. Growing up, if my mom was ever wondering if we'd be fussy about dinner, she'd at least know there was always, always vermicelli rice with laban (plain whole-milk yogurt) on the table. It's everyone's favorite! By the way, the kind of vermicelli I buy at the Middle Eastern store is already broken up into one-inch pieces— if the vermicelli you find isn't, you can just break it into one-inch pieces yourself.

2 cups long-grain white rice

2 tablespoons olive oil

½ cup vermicelli

½ teaspoon salt

Pinch of ground cinnamon
(optional)

1. Rinse the rice in a fine-mesh sieve with cold water until the water runs clear. Drain well and set aside.

2. Heat the oil in a large pot over medium heat. Add the vermicelli and toast, stirring frequently, until the pasta is a deep golden-brown color, 2 to 4 minutes.

3. Add the rice on top of the toasted vermicelli. Stir until everything is combined and coated with the oil. Season with the salt. Add 4 cups of water and bring everything to a boil over high heat. Reduce the heat to low, cover with a tight-fitting lid, and cook for 15 minutes.

4. Remove the pot from the heat and let it rest, covered, for 5 minutes longer. Uncover and season with cinnamon (if using). Fluff with a fork and serve warm.

Turmeric Cashew Rice

Serves 8 | Active Time: 15 minutes | Total Time: 40 minutes

Growing up, we ate a lot of rice—my mom would make a pot of rice at least once a week. But if I ever saw nuts on top of that rice (usually a mix of almonds, cashews, and pine nuts), I knew it was a special occasion. Nuts are often used to decorate the dish, taking something day-to-day and turning it into something celebratory. Now, if that rice had nuts and *it was yellow? That right there was a level-ten special occasion! Thankfully, this dish feels extra special without taking much extra time. And it's as welcome at Tuesday dinner as it is at a holiday spread.*

2 cups long-grain white rice

2 tablespoons (¼ stick) **unsalted butter,** divided

1 cup cashews

1 small yellow onion, finely chopped

1 tablespoon ground turmeric

½ teaspoon ground ginger

½ teaspoon salt

1. Rinse the rice in a fine-mesh sieve with cold water until the water runs clear. Drain well and set aside.

2. Heat 1 tablespoon of the butter in a large pot over medium heat. Add the cashews and toast, stirring frequently, until they're golden brown and fragrant, 3 to 5 minutes. Transfer to a bowl and set aside.

3. Heat the remaining 1 tablespoon of butter in the same pot over medium heat. Add the onion and cook, stirring occasionally, until softened, about 5 minutes. Add the rice on top of the cooked onion. Season with the turmeric, ginger, and salt. Continue cooking, stirring frequently, until the rice smells toasted and is coated with the spices, about 2 minutes longer.

4. Add 3 cups of water and bring the mixture to a boil over high heat. Reduce the heat to low, cover with a tight-fitting lid, and cook for 15 minutes.

5. Remove the pot from the heat and let it rest, covered, for 5 minutes longer. Uncover and fluff with a fork. Serve warm, sprinkled with the cashews.

Tomato Rice Pilaf

Serves 8 | Active Time: 15 minutes | Total Time: 35 minutes

If these side dishes seem skewed in the rice direction, it's because they are. Rice is the number-one side dish we ate growing up, and it's indispensable to so many regions of the Mediterranean, especially the Eastern Mediterranean. If Mom was grilling beef skewers, roasting chicken thighs, or simmering a stew, we knew rice would be served alongside it. As a mom myself now, I'm often adding rice to meals to increase the balance and satisfaction. This rice pilaf is one of my favorites because of its distinguished color and wonderful flavor. It also feels like a throwback to an African tomato-based rice dish called jollof rice that my mom made all the time when we lived in Sierra Leone.

2 cups basmati rice

2 tablespoons olive oil

1 yellow onion, finely chopped

3 garlic cloves, minced

¼ cup tomato paste

½ teaspoon Seven Spice (page 259 or store-bought)

½ teaspoon salt

¼ teaspoon crushed red pepper

1 cup finely chopped Roma tomatoes (about 2)

1. Rinse the rice in a fine-mesh sieve with cold water until the water runs clear. Drain well and set aside.

2. Heat the oil in a large pot over medium heat. Add the onion and cook, stirring occasionally, until softened, about 5 minutes. Add the garlic and cook, stirring constantly, until fragrant, about 30 seconds longer. Stir in the rice, tomato paste, seven spice, salt, and crushed red pepper. Cook, stirring occasionally, until the rice smells toasted and is thoroughly coated in the tomato paste, about 2 minutes longer.

3. Stir in the tomatoes and 3 cups of water. Bring everything to a boil over high heat, then reduce the heat to low, cover with a tight-fitting lid, and cook for 15 minutes.

4. Remove the pot from the heat and let it rest, covered, for 5 minutes longer. Uncover, fluff with a fork, and serve warm.

Sumac Sweet Potato Wedges

Serves 4 | Active Time: 10 minutes | Total Time: 30 minutes

Sweet potatoes aren't really typical to the Mediterranean, but they sure are popular in the Midwest! And they just happen to be one of my favorite root vegetables. I love giving sweet potato wedges a classic Mediterranean treatment with olive oil, garlic, and tart-fresh sumac and pairing with my super-quick Tahini Sauce (page 256) for dipping.

4 medium sweet potatoes, cut into 8 wedges each

¼ cup olive oil

2 teaspoons ground sumac

2 teaspoons garlic powder

1 teaspoon salt, plus more to taste

½ teaspoon black pepper

Tahini Sauce, for serving (optional; page 256)

1. Preheat the oven to 425°F. Line a large baking sheet with parchment paper.

2. On the prepared baking sheet, toss the sweet potatoes with the oil, sumac, garlic powder, salt, and pepper until evenly coated. Arrange the wedges in a single layer and bake, flipping once halfway through, until browned and tender, 30 to 35 minutes.

3. Right when the wedges come out of the oven, season them with more salt. Serve with the Tahini Sauce for dipping (if using).

Cumin-Spiced Carrots

Serves 4 | Active Time: 10 minutes | Total Time: 40 minutes

When we would vacation in Lebanon during the summer, I remember having the best snack at the beach: sliced raw carrots with sea salt, cumin, and lemon juice. These cold, crisp carrots had the perfect crunch and the freshest flavor! I wanted to lick my lemony fingers after every bite. This recipe is inspired by that nostalgic beach snack, except I add olive oil and roast the carrots in the oven until they're deeply browned and tender.

2 pounds carrots, peeled and sliced diagonally into ½-inch pieces

2 tablespoons olive oil

1½ teaspoons ground cumin

½ teaspoon salt

½ teaspoon black pepper

2 tablespoons lemon juice

1. Preheat the oven to 425°F. Line a large baking sheet with parchment paper.

2. On the prepared baking sheet, toss the carrots, oil, cumin, salt, and pepper until evenly coated. Spread the carrots in a single layer, then roast until fork-tender and caramelized, 25 to 30 minutes.

3. Right when the carrots come out of the oven, toss them with the lemon juice and serve.

Couscous-Almond Pilaf with Dates

Serves 8 | Active Time: 15 minutes | Total Time: 25 minutes

As much rice as we eat, sometimes I just don't have the time at the end of a long day to wait for a pot of rice to cook before taking the kids to soccer or piano lessons. That's when couscous comes into play! There are actually three types of couscous, all of which I use regularly. My favorite for quick meals, though, is fine couscous. Because it's steamed and dried before it's packaged, all you need to do is rehydrate it with boiling water or stock and let it rest, covered, for five minutes. How about that for a five-minute side dish? And if I have six minutes, I like to zhuzh it up with nuts and dried fruit, like the almonds and dates in this recipe. Here, I'm taking a slightly more scenic route by using the couscous as the base of a fragrant, delicious pilaf.

½ cup **slivered almonds**

1 tablespoon **olive oil**

1 medium **yellow onion,** finely chopped

½ **teaspoon salt**

½ **teaspoon black pepper**

2 cups **fine couscous**

¼ **cup chopped fresh dill,** plus more for serving

2 cups **vegetable broth**

12 **Medjool dates,** pitted and chopped

1. Heat a dry large pot over medium heat. Add the almonds and toast, stirring frequently, until fragrant and golden, about 5 minutes. Transfer the almonds to a small bowl and set aside.

2. To the same pot, add the oil, onion, salt, and pepper. Cook, stirring occasionally, until the onion is softened and slightly golden, 6 to 8 minutes. Stir in the couscous and dill. Toast, stirring frequently, for about 2 minutes.

3. Add the broth, increase the heat to medium-high, and bring everything to a rapid simmer. Turn off the heat, cover the pot with a tight-fitting lid, and let it sit for 5 minutes. Uncover and fluff with a fork. Stir in the dates. Serve warm, scattered with the almonds and more dill.

Spicy Chickpea Skillet

Serves 4 | Active Time: 15 minutes | Total Time: 15 minutes

I love balila, a Lebanese dish of warm chickpeas with cumin and olive oil that's usually eaten for breakfast or brunch. I love it so much, as a matter of fact, that I asked myself, How can I eat my favorite cozy, comforting chickpea dish at any hour of the day? The answer: make it deeply savory, get it all browned and toasty in a skillet, and embrace the opportunity to deck out humble canned chickpeas with some spice! This balila-inspired recipe is by no means traditional, but wow is it incredible alongside any of the seafood or meat mains from this book—or with just some warm pita for dipping.

2 tablespoons olive oil

2 (15-ounce) **cans chickpeas,** drained and rinsed

1 teaspoon ground cumin

½ teaspoon salt

2 tablespoons harissa paste

1 cup jarred roasted red peppers, chopped

1 teaspoon red wine vinegar

¼ cup chopped fresh cilantro

1. Heat the oil in a large nonstick skillet over medium-high heat. Add the chickpeas, cumin, and salt. Cook, stirring occasionally, until the chickpeas start to brown, 4 to 6 minutes.

2. Add the harissa and cook, stirring constantly, until fragrant and caramelized, about 30 seconds. Add the red peppers and cook, stirring occasionally and scraping up any browned bits from the bottom of the skillet, until warmed through, about 2 minutes longer.

3. Remove the skillet from the heat. Stir in the vinegar, scatter with the cilantro, and serve.

Batata Harra

Serves 4 | Active Time: 10 minutes | Total Time: 60 minutes

With a name that literally translates to "spicy potatoes," know that these potatoes pack some heat. Luckily, if you're not a fan of spicy things, you can still make this recipe and omit the crushed red pepper—or substitute one teaspoon of black pepper for a subtler kick. These potatoes are the most famous potatoes in Lebanon. They're loved for their fiery flavor, crispy texture, and the fresh garlicky cilantro mixture they're coated in. (Yes, there's a whole cup of cilantro in this recipe, and that's not a typo, my friends! So good.) They're traditionally deep-fried, but I find that baking them at a high oven temperature with plenty of olive oil gives me the texture I'm after with less cleanup.

8 medium yellow potatoes, peeled and cut into 1-inch cubes

3 tablespoons olive oil, divided

½ teaspoon salt

3 garlic cloves, minced

1 teaspoon crushed red pepper

1 cup fresh cilantro, chopped, divided

Lemon wedges, for serving

1. Preheat the oven to 450°F. Line a large baking sheet with parchment paper.

2. On the prepared baking sheet, toss the potatoes with 2 tablespoons of the oil and the salt. Arrange them in a single layer and roast, stirring once halfway through, until golden brown and crisp, 50 to 55 minutes.

3. Meanwhile, heat the remaining 1 tablespoon of oil in a small skillet over medium heat. Add the garlic, crushed red pepper, and most of the cilantro. Cook, stirring constantly, until the garlic is golden, about 2 minutes. Remove the skillet from the heat.

4. Right when the potatoes come out of the oven, add the cilantro mixture on top and toss well. Garnish with the remaining cilantro and serve with the lemon wedges.

Lemon-Feta Broccoli

Serves 4 | Active Time: 15 minutes | Total Time: 15 minutes

How nice is crisp-tender, bright green broccoli? If you cook it just right, it maintains its subtly sweet and grassy flavor, which I like to highlight with two of my favorite ingredients: fresh lemon and salty feta. And definitely save those broccoli stalks! I like to trim the woody ends and peel them like I would a carrot—then I can thinly slice them to add to salads, stir-fries, or trays of roasted veggies.

2 heads broccoli, cut into florets

2 tablespoons olive oil

2 garlic cloves, grated

Zest and juice of ½ lemon

¼ teaspoon salt

¼ teaspoon black pepper

¼ cup crumbled feta cheese

½ teaspoon zaatar

1. Bring a pot of salted water to a boil over high heat. Add the broccoli and cook until bright green and fork-tender, 2 to 3 minutes. Drain and run under cold water to stop the cooking—give the strainer a shake to get rid of excess moisture. Set aside.

2. Heat the oil in a large skillet over medium heat. Add the garlic and cook, stirring constantly, until fragrant, about 30 seconds. Add the reserved broccoli and toss to coat. Cook until the broccoli is just warmed through, about 1 minute. Remove the skillet from the heat. Stir in the lemon zest, lemon juice, salt, and pepper. Sprinkle the feta and zaatar over the top and serve immediately.

Tahini-Glazed Cauliflower

Serves 4 | Active Time: 10 minutes | Total Time: 40 minutes

Cauliflower and tahini are an iconic combo in Mediterranean cooking. Whenever my mom makes Tahini Sauce (page 256), she makes a large batch to serve with tons of different dishes. Her favorite is always roasted cauliflower with tahini wrapped in pita. Inspired by her delicious wrap, I wanted to recreate those flavors in a side dish that goes with everything—it can even stand alone as the main attraction. So, I tossed cauliflower florets with a generous amount of tahini, lemon, and spices and roasted it. The result is something Mama would definitely give two thumbs up to.

¼ **cup tahini**

3 **tablespoons lemon juice**

1 **teaspoon ground cumin**

½ **teaspoon paprika**

½ **teaspoon salt**

½ **teaspoon black pepper**

1 **large head cauliflower,** cut into florets

1. Preheat the oven to 425°F. Line a large baking sheet with parchment paper.

2. In a large bowl, whisk the tahini, lemon juice, cumin, paprika, salt, and pepper until it forms a thick paste. Whisk in 2 tablespoons of water until smooth. Add the cauliflower florets and toss until they're well coated.

3. Using tongs, arrange the florets evenly spaced in a single layer on the prepared baking sheet. Roast, undisturbed, until fork-tender and golden brown, about 30 minutes.

9

Snacks & Condiments

No-Bake Oat Bites

Makes 20 to 24 bites | Active Time: 15 minutes | Total Time: 15 minutes

I think a perfect snack for instant energy is a palmful of nuts and dried fruit. That's why I turn again and again to these oat bites, which take sweet, chewy figs and mix them up with an extra nutritional boost from oats, peanut butter, and flaxseeds. The best thing about these bites is how flexible they are. If you want to use sunflower or almond butter instead of peanut butter, be my guest! Prefer raisins or chopped dates to figs? I like your style!

1 cup no-stir peanut butter

⅓ cup honey

1 teaspoon ground cinnamon

2 cups quick-cooking rolled oats

1 cup dried figs, chopped

½ cup ground flaxseed

1. In a medium bowl, mix the peanut butter, honey, and cinnamon until smooth. Stir in the oats, figs, and flaxseed until everything is incorporated and has come together into a sticky ball.

2. Using a medium spring-loaded cookie scoop, scoop and roll about 1½ tablespoons of the mixture into a small ball and place in a storage container. Repeat with the remaining mixture. Store in the fridge for up to 2 weeks.

Brownie Date Balls

Makes 12 balls | Active Time: 10 minutes | Total Time: 10 minutes

These brownie date balls taste and feel like decadent chocolate truffles, but they're packed with fiber and energy from delicious dates. I like using Medjool dates best because of their plush, soft texture, but if your dates have hardened during storage, just soak them in hot water for ten minutes, then drain and pat them dry before using. These brownie date balls are great for snacking or for a sweet bite after dinner.

1 cup walnuts

1 cup pitted Medjool dates

⅓ cup chocolate chips

¼ cup cocoa powder

1 teaspoon vanilla extract

Salt

1. Pulse the walnuts in a food processor until finely ground. Add the dates, chocolate chips, cocoa powder, vanilla, and a pinch of salt. Process, scraping down the sides as needed, until you have a soft, sticky ball of dough.

2. Using a medium spring-loaded cookie scoop, scoop and roll about 1½ tablespoons of the mixture into a ball and place in a storage container. Repeat with the remaining mixture. Store in the fridge for up to 2 weeks.

Almond Coconut Bars

Makes 16 bars | Active Time: 10 minutes | Total Time: 25 minutes

These bars are a cross between an energy bar and a thick, chewy cookie. They kind of remind me of basbousa, a coconut-and-almond cake from Egypt, but they also look like blondies—another great Eastern Mediterranean and Midwestern mash-up. I also love that these bars are flourless, fuss-free, and basically failproof, so you can whip them up in no time to satisfy a sweets craving. Since they travel well, they're great for school lunch boxes, hikes, and field trips, too.

1 cup almond butter

½ cup honey

1 teaspoon vanilla extract

2 cups almond flour

1 cup plus 2 tablespoons unsweetened shredded coconut, divided

½ teaspoon baking soda

1. Preheat the oven to 350°F. Line an 8 × 8-inch baking dish with parchment paper, leaving about 2 inches of extra parchment over both sides.

2. In a large bowl, mix the almond butter, honey, and vanilla until smooth. Add the almond flour, 1 cup of the coconut, and the baking soda. Mix to a soft, smooth dough—it will look like a shaggy pie crust at first, then come together into a ball as you continue to mix.

3. Press the almond-coconut batter into the prepared baking dish, then sprinkle the remaining 2 tablespoons of coconut over the top. Bake until puffed and lightly browned on top, 14 to 16 minutes.

4. Cool in the pan for 10 minutes, then transfer to a wire rack and cool completely before slicing into 16 bars. Store in the fridge for up to 2 weeks.

Pecan Date Bars

Makes 16 bars | Active Time: 25 minutes | Total Time: 55 minutes

We love a bar in the Midwest, and a super common version is an oatmeal bar filled with strawberry preserves. These oat-and-pecan-packed date bars are a Mediterranean riff on that classic recipe, with a chewy, buttery crust, a perfect crumb topping, and the easiest homemade date caramel filling. They've been on my website for many years, and it has been so fun and fulfilling to read how well loved they are. People have shared them with neighbors during the holidays, topped them with whipped cream to serve for a dinner party, eaten them with cardamom-spiced coffee, and even used them as the inspiration to get into the kitchen for the first time—my heart!

Filling

1½ cups chopped pitted Medjool dates

1 tablespoon lemon juice

½ cup pecans, finely chopped

Base

1½ cups all-purpose flour

1 cup rolled oats

⅔ cup (packed) **dark brown sugar**

½ teaspoon ground cinnamon

½ teaspoon baking soda

½ teaspoon salt

½ cup (1 stick) **unsalted butter,** melted

1. Preheat the oven to 350°F. Line an 8 × 8-inch baking dish with parchment paper, leaving about 2 inches of extra parchment over both sides.

2. In a small saucepan, bring 1¼ cups of water to a boil over high heat. Add the dates and boil, stirring occasionally, until the liquid has evaporated and the dates have melted and thickened, about 5 minutes. Remove the pan from the heat; stir in the lemon juice and pecans. Set aside to cool for 10 minutes.

3. In a large bowl, whisk the flour, oats, sugar, cinnamon, baking soda, and salt. Pour the melted butter on top. Using your fingertips, rub the butter into the flour mixture until you have a pebbly texture with moist pea-size clumps.

4. Press half of the flour mixture evenly and firmly over the bottom of the prepared baking dish. Spread the date mixture evenly over the top. Sprinkle the remaining flour mixture over the date mixture; press gently to help the crumbs adhere.

5. Bake until the top and edges are golden brown, 35 to 40 minutes. Transfer the baking dish to a wire rack and cool completely. Cut into 16 bars and serve. Store the bars, tightly sealed, at room temperature for 3 days or in the fridge for up to 1 week.

Apricot Cardamom Granola

Makes about 8 cups | Active Time: 10 minutes | Total Time: 55 minutes

Granola preferences seem to be a personal thing, and here's my version of perfection: sweet-and-chewy apricots, nutty tahini, a hint of cardamom, and thick pieces that aren't too coarse or too crumbly. You might be surprised by how simple it is to make homemade granola, and this recipe makes a nice, large batch for breakfast or snacking. It's so good on its own, but you can also try it with some almond milk or Greek yogurt and fresh fruit.

½ **cup tahini**

½ **cup maple syrup**

2 tablespoons (¼ stick) **unsalted butter,** melted

1 teaspoon vanilla extract

¼ **teaspoon salt**

3 cups rolled oats

1 cup diced dried apricots

½ **cup sesame seeds**

1 teaspoon ground cardamom

1. Preheat the oven to 325°F. Line a large baking sheet with parchment paper.

2. In a small bowl, whisk the tahini, maple syrup, butter, vanilla, and salt until smooth. Stir in the oats, apricots, sesame seeds, and cardamom.

3. Evenly spread the mixture on the prepared baking sheet. Bake for 20 minutes.

4. Remove the granola from the oven, give it a stir, and then flatten it once more into a single layer. Continue baking until golden brown and very fragrant, 15 to 20 minutes longer.

5. Let the granola cool completely, undisturbed, on the baking sheet. Break into chunks with your hands and store, tightly sealed, in a jar for up to 1 month.

Rose Water Fruit Salad

Makes 9 cups | Active Time: 20 minutes | Total Time: 20 minutes

Subtly floral fruit salad is a great way to use up a surplus of ripe fruit and repurpose it into something beautiful and delicious. This fruit salad with a hint of rose water is a common snack that my mom, relatives, and friends make for visitors. It's timeless and truly wonderful any time of year when I want something healthy, simple, and sweet to serve guests. What makes this Middle Eastern–style fruit salad extra special, besides the rose water, are the nuts folded into it. I like almonds, pistachios, or even pine nuts. Lastly, make sure to dice all of the fruit into small half-inch cubes so that everything can be scooped up with a spoon—kind of elegant, right?

2 cups hulled and diced strawberries

2 cups diced pineapple

2 mangoes, diced

4 kiwis, diced

1 apple, cored and diced

½ cup slivered almonds

½ cup shelled pistachios

½ cup orange juice

1 tablespoon rose water

1. In a large serving bowl, add the strawberries, pineapple, mangoes, kiwis, apple, almonds, and pistachios.

2. Pour the orange juice and rose water over the top and gently toss to combine.

3. Serve immediately at room temperature or chill in the fridge for up to 1 hour.

Pickled Turnips

Makes 1 (32-ounce) jar | Active Time: 10 minutes | Total Time: 10 minutes (plus 5 days for pickling)

These pickled turnips are a staple in home kitchens of the Eastern Mediterranean. Crunchy, tangy, and the brightest pink you can imagine, they're scattered on salads, layered into classic sandwiches like My Favorite Chicken Shawarma (page 210), and piled next to plates of Baba's Classic Hummus (page 66) and Crispy Falafel (page 156). My fridge is never without them! Just remember that, though preparing these pickles takes just ten minutes of hands-on time, they'll need five full days in the fridge to reach the right texture and flavor—so plan your pickle cravings accordingly!

1½ cups boiling water

½ cup white vinegar

1 tablespoon salt

1 tablespoon sugar

1 garlic clove, smashed

2 bay leaves

2 medium turnips, peeled and cut into ½-inch batons or wedges

1 small beet, peeled and quartered

1. Add the water, vinegar, salt, sugar, garlic, and bay leaves to a 32-ounce wide-mouth glass jar. Stir continuously until the salt and sugar dissolve.

2. Add the turnips and beets to the jar, making sure everything is submerged in the vinegar mixture (top off the jar with a little water, if needed). Let cool completely, uncovered, to room temperature.

3. When cool, tightly seal the jar and give everything a shake to distribute the beet juice. Refrigerate, unopened, for 5 days. After 5 days, the pickles can be opened and enjoyed for up to 1 month.

Pickled Red Onions

Makes 1 (32-ounce) jar | Active Time: 10 minutes | Total Time: 10 minutes (plus cooling time)

There's a quick way to pickle onions, a staple condiment in Mediterranean cuisine— and for this busy mama, you know it's the method I always fall back on. These onions are ready within an hour of preparation and keep for about a month in the fridge, which means no waiting for weeks to eat them, no simmering jars in pots of water for sterilization, and no delayed enjoyment of these bright, flavorful powerhouses that add a fun pop of color to so many meals. Try them on top of a Cheesy Squash Omelet (page 55), tucked into my Tahini & Smashed Avocado Chicken Sandwich (page 127), or scattered over a delicious roast, like my Yogurt & Rosemary Roasted Chicken Thighs (page 201). They're salty, sweet, sour, and refreshingly crisp.

2 small red onions, thinly sliced

1½ cups red wine vinegar

¼ cup granulated sugar

1½ teaspoons salt

2 bay leaves

½ teaspoon whole black peppercorns

1. Place the onions in a 32-ounce wide-mouth glass jar. Set aside.

2. In a small saucepan, bring the vinegar, sugar, salt, bay leaves, peppercorns, and 1 cup of water to a boil over high heat. Stir a few times to dissolve the sugar.

3. Pour the boiling vinegar mixture over the onions, ensuring that all the onions are submerged (top off the jar with a little water, if needed). Let cool completely, uncovered, to room temperature. Use immediately or tightly seal and store in the fridge for up to 1 month.

Tahini Sauce

Makes about 1 cup | Active Time: 10 minutes | Total Time: 10 minutes

By now you've seen me mention "Tahini Sauce, for serving" about a million times. What can I say? It's essential and always invited! It's amazing that this sauce is only made with four ingredients because it instantly adds so much flavor to everything. I always have it on hand for Crispy Falafel (page 156), Mama's Beef Shawarma (page 213), and my Tahini Kafta (page 214). But really, with this tahini sauce recipe in your back pocket, there are so many delicious meals at your fingertips—try rubbing it over chicken or fish before roasting, tossing it with crisp lettuce like romaine as a simple salad dressing, or using it as a dip for fresh vegetables.

½ **cup tahini**

⅓ **cup lemon juice,** plus more as needed

2 garlic cloves, finely grated

¼ **teaspoon salt,** plus more as needed

1. In a small bowl, whisk the tahini, lemon juice, garlic, and salt until it forms a thick paste.

2. Add ¼ cup of water and whisk until the tahini sauce is creamy and pourable. If necessary, add more water 1 tablespoon at a time, as needed.

3. Taste and adjust the seasoning by adding more lemon juice or salt, if needed. Store in the fridge for up to 1 week.

Cucumber Yogurt Sauce

Makes 1 generous cup | Active Time: 10 minutes | Total Time: 10 minutes

This yogurt sauce is rich and refreshing at the same time, with creamy yogurt, crispy Persian cucumber, savory garlic, and dried mint. It's an ideal way to top off a meal with something simple and special or to cool off a piping hot dish for hungry kiddos. It's a classic accompaniment to recipes like Mujadara (page 167) or Spiced Couscous-Stuffed Peppers (page 175), but it's also so versatile that I've been known to use it as a dressing for crispy lettuce or warm roasted potatoes.

1 cup plain yogurt

1 Persian cucumber, diced

1 garlic clove, finely grated

1 teaspoon dried mint, plus more as needed

¼ teaspoon salt, plus more as needed

1. In a small bowl, stir the yogurt, cucumber, garlic, mint, and salt. Taste and adjust the seasoning as needed. If you prefer a more pourable sauce, you can thin it by stirring in ¼ cup of water.

2. Serve immediately or transfer to a storage container and store in the fridge for up to 1 week.

Labneh

Makes about 2 cups   Active Time: 10 minutes   Total Time: 10 minutes (plus 2 days for straining)

Labneh—one of my eight Mediterranean staples (see page 18) and something my fridge is never, ever without—is actually a cinch to make at home. My sister doesn't cook much, but even she makes it from scratch, straining the yogurt for a couple of days while she goes about life. And that's what labneh is, really: plain yogurt that has been strained to remove most of its whey until you're left with a rich, velvety, cream cheese–like texture that's truly irresistible. I mean, if you've cooked your way through this book to this point, you've already seen labneh in sauces, in soups, in salad dressings . . . you two go way back by now! Try it as a béchamel-like base in my White Zucchini Pizza with Garlicky Labneh (page 171), or as a zesty vinaigrette in my Roasted Chickpea Salad with Labneh Dressing (page 107). Of course, you can also slather it on Zaatar Manakeesh (page 43), which is a common way to enjoy it. So good!

32 ounces (about 4 cups) **plain whole-milk yogurt**

½ teaspoon salt

1. Line a large fine-mesh sieve with a double layer of cheesecloth with at least 4 inches of overhang. Set over a medium bowl.

2. Pour the yogurt into the cheesecloth. Sprinkle with the salt and carefully stir to incorporate. Tie the ends of the cheesecloth up over the yogurt; you want the yogurt to be completely concealed. Set the whole thing—the yogurt in the cheesecloth in the sieve in the bowl—in the fridge for 24 to 48 hours, depending on how thick you like your labneh. (The longer it rests, the more whey will drain from the yogurt, and the thicker the resulting labneh will be.)

3. Carefully unwrap the labneh from the cheesecloth and transfer it to a clean bowl or storage container (discard the leftover liquid in the bowl). The labneh should be thick but spreadable and will keep in the fridge, tightly sealed, for up to 2 weeks.

Seven Spice

Makes about ⅓ cup | Active Time: 5 minutes | Total Time: 5 minutes

I'm sure you and seven spice are close at this point! It's one of my eight Mediterranean staples, after all (see page 16). Savory, warming, and scented with hints of sweetness thanks to spices like cinnamon, nutmeg, and cloves, this spice blend is the perfect way to build flavor with minimal effort. It's the secret oomph *behind my Roasted Chickpea Salad with Labneh Dressing (page 107), indispensable in my Seven Spice Roast Chicken & Pomegranate Potatoes (page 202), and responsible for the seriously good flavor of my Tomato Rice Pilaf (page 226), among many other recipes. You can purchase seven spice online, but guess what—it couldn't be faster or easier to make at home with just seven preground spices.*

1 tablespoon ground allspice

1 tablespoon ground coriander

1 tablespoon ground cinnamon

1½ teaspoons black pepper

1½ teaspoons ground cloves

1½ teaspoons ground cumin

1½ teaspoons ground nutmeg

In a small bowl, mix the allspice, coriander, cinnamon, pepper, cloves, cumin, and nutmeg with a spoon until well combined. Store, tightly sealed, in a small jar or airtight container for up to 6 months.

Toum

Makes about 3 cups | Active Time: 25 minutes | Total Time: 25 minutes

Here's the crazy thing about this Lebanese garlic sauce—it goes from cloves to clouds like magic! Truly. You just blend garlic with salt, oil, and lemon juice, and it all turns into a fluffy, spreadable dip that's addictively good over everything. You might think three cups of garlic sauce is too much, but I think you'll change your mind when you find yourself slathering it on My Favorite Chicken Shawarma (page 210), Lemon-Dill Tuna Patties (page 197), or Crispy Rice & Shrimp (page 190). Besides, it lasts up to three months in the fridge. You'll notice that I recommend removing any green sprouts before blending. It's a fiddly extra step, but it's so worth it—it provides the freshest flavor with none of that hot garlic spice. If you're short on time, though, your garlic sauce will just pack a little extra punch!

1 cup peeled garlic cloves

2 teaspoons kosher salt

2½ cups neutral oil, such as canola oil, divided

⅓ cup lemon juice, divided

1. Slice the garlic cloves in half lengthwise and peel any green stems from the center.

2. In a food processor, process the garlic and salt until the garlic is finely minced and almost paste-like, about 30 seconds, scraping down the sides as needed.

3. With the food processor running, slowly stream in 2 tablespoons of the oil. Stop to scrape down the bowl. Repeat this process, 2 tablespoons of oil at a time, about three more times, until the garlic sauce has doubled in size and starts to look creamy and fluffy—this means the garlic sauce is emulsifying, making it harder to break.

4. With the food processor running, slowly stream in ½ cup of the oil. Next, slowly stream in half of the lemon juice, then slowly stream in another ½ cup of oil. Repeat with the remaining lemon juice and 1 cup of oil, stopping to scrape the bowl as needed. This will take 10 to 15 minutes to complete, and your patience will pay off.

5. Transfer the toum to a storage container with a fitted lid. Cover the container first with a paper towel (to absorb excess moisture), then secure the lid on top. Store the toum in the fridge, but remove the paper towel from the container after 24 hours. Continue to refrigerate the toum for up to 3 months.

10

Desserts & Drinks

Olive Oil Cake

Serves 8 | Active Time: 10 minutes | Total Time: 45 minutes

This easy, versatile, and delightful olive oil cake was the first recipe from the Feel Good Foodie cooking challenges I started years ago. I wanted to encourage my community to cook and bake together, and there's no better place to start than a one-bowl cake! Some people were surprised by the use of olive oil instead of butter in this cake and were excited to learn that baking with olive oil is common in many Mediterranean desserts. Hundreds of people got to baking this tender, perfectly sweetened olive oil cake in just one month, and it's now the most popular dessert on my website. (As I write this book, it has thousands of five-star reviews!) It's so simple yet so impressive and one of the best cake recipes to have in your back pocket. It's perfect alone with a cup of tea or coffee and also pretty great midmorning with a spoonful of Greek yogurt and some fresh raspberries.

⅔ **cup olive oil,** plus more for coating the pan

1¼ **cups all-purpose flour**

⅔ **cup granulated sugar**

½ **teaspoon baking powder**

¼ **teaspoon baking soda**

¼ **teaspoon salt**

½ **cup whole-milk Greek yogurt**

2 **large eggs**

Zest of 1 lemon plus 3 tablespoons lemon juice

1. Preheat the oven to 350°F. Generously oil a 9-inch round cake pan.

2. In a large bowl, whisk the flour, sugar, baking powder, baking soda, and salt.

3. Create a wide well in the center of the dry ingredients; add the oil, yogurt, and eggs. Carefully whisk the wet ingredients together, then gradually whisk the dry ingredients into the wet ingredients until no streaks of flour remain. Stir in the lemon zest and juice.

4. Pour the batter into the prepared pan. Bake until the top is golden brown and springy and a toothpick inserted in the center comes out clean, 30 to 35 minutes. Cool for at least 15 minutes before slicing and serving.

Easy Walnut Baklava

Makes 18 pieces   Active Time: 20 minutes   Total Time: 1 hour 20 minutes

Baklava is the ultimate sign of celebration in my family and in the Middle East, especially during our Eid holidays. When I was growing up, my mom used to make baklava by layering one sheet of phyllo at a time, carefully brushing each fragile layer with butter. I remember nervously watching her work quickly yet gently so the whole surface of the phyllo could be covered with butter before it dried out or cracked. When we moved to Dearborn, Michigan, we were lucky to be near some of the best baklava bakeries in the country, and my mom never made baklava again. But when I eventually moved away from Dearborn, I craved that baklava ideal: flaky, buttery, a little floral, perfectly sweet, and nutty. I finally decided to give it a go myself and—wondering if I could save a few steps in the painstaking process—discovered this pretty fast foolproof method. It's seriously delicious, and only take about twenty minutes of your time.

Simple Syrup

¾ **cup granulated sugar**

1 **tablespoon lemon juice**

1 **tablespoon orange blossom water**

Filling and Assembly

3 **cups unsalted raw walnuts**

½ **cup granulated sugar**

¾ **cup clarified butter or ghee,** melted, plus more for brushing

1 (16-ounce) **box 9 × 14-inch phyllo dough sheets,** at room temperature, trimmed to fit baking dish

Chopped pistachios, for garnish

1. To make the simple syrup, in a small saucepan over medium-high heat, combine the sugar, lemon juice, and ½ cup of water. Bring the mixture to a boil, then reduce the heat to medium-low. Simmer, stirring occasionally, until the sugar has dissolved and the mixture is clear and slightly reduced, 5 to 7 minutes. Remove from heat and add the orange blossom water. Set aside.

2. In a food processor, add the walnuts and sugar. Pulse until the nuts are coarsely chopped. Set aside.

3. Preheat the oven to 350°F. Generously brush the bottom of a 9 × 13-inch baking dish with the butter.

4. Lay about two-thirds of the phyllo sheets in the baking dish. Spread all of the sugared nuts evenly on top in a single layer. Lay the remaining one-third of the phyllo sheets on top.

5. Carefully cut the baklava into diamonds by making four cuts lengthwise and eight cuts crosswise on the diagonal, holding down the phyllo sheets with your other hand to keep everything steady. Evenly pour the butter over the top. Let sit for 5 minutes to allow the butter to soak in.

6. Bake until the baklava is golden brown all the way into the cut lines, 50 to 60 minutes.

7. Remove the baklava from the oven and immediately pour the cooled simple syrup evenly over the top. Let the baklava cool completely to room temperature, about 2 hours, garnish with pistachios, and serve.

One-Bowl Oatmeal Chocolate Chunk Cookies

Makes about 2 dozen cookies   Active Time: 20 minutes   Total Time: 30 minutes

These chewy oatmeal chocolate chunk cookies are going to be your new favorites. They come together in a single bowl, are infused with a subtle hint of cinnamon, and have the best-ever chewy texture, even days after baking. With this recipe, there is no pile of mixing bowls, no chilling the dough, and no need to delay a cookie craving. All wins in my book!

½ **cup** (1 stick) **unsalted butter,** at room temperature

1 cup (packed) **light brown sugar**

¼ **cup granulated sugar**

1 large egg plus 1 large egg yolk

2 teaspoons ground cinnamon

1 teaspoon vanilla extract

¾ **teaspoon baking soda**

⅛ **teaspoon salt**

1¼ **cups all-purpose flour**

1 cup rolled oats

3 ounces dark chocolate, chopped

1. Position a rack in the center of the oven and preheat the oven to 350°F. Line two baking sheets with parchment paper.

2. Using an electric hand mixer on medium speed, cream the butter, brown sugar, and granulated sugar in a large bowl until completely incorporated, about 3 minutes. Beat in the egg, egg yolk, cinnamon, vanilla, baking soda, and salt until completely smooth, about 1 minute.

3. Using a wooden spoon, stir in the flour and oats until no streaks of flour remain. Fold in the chocolate.

4. Using a medium spring-loaded cookie scoop, scoop about 1½ tablespoons of the dough and place it on one of the prepared baking sheets. Repeat with the remaining cookie dough, making sure the cookies are spaced at least 2 inches apart.

5. Bake the cookies until they're golden brown and firm around the edges, 9 to 11 minutes. Cool the cookies on the baking sheets before enjoying.

Cherry Chocolate Chia Pudding

Serves 2 | Active Time: 5 minutes | Total Time: 5 minutes (plus chilling)

This just-sweet-enough dark chocolate chia pudding is great for those days I want something sweet but nutrient dense. Chia seeds are tiny-but-mighty nutritional powerhouses packed with omega-3 fatty acids, protein, carbohydrates, healthy fats, fiber, and antioxidants. Even better, they're so delicious and satisfying when soaked until thick and creamy with cherries, chocolate chips, and a pretty perfect balance of maple syrup and cocoa. This recipe is a chameleon that can qualify as a snack or as a dessert!

1 cup almond milk

⅓ cup chia seeds

¼ cup cocoa powder

2 tablespoons maple syrup

⅛ teaspoon salt

⅓ cup pitted cherries
(fresh or frozen), chopped

2 tablespoons chocolate chips

1. In a medium bowl or storage container, vigorously whisk the milk, chia seeds, cocoa powder, maple syrup, and salt, incorporating any cocoa powder sticking to the sides and bottom. Stir in the cherries and chocolate chips.

2. Cover the chia pudding and refrigerate until thick and creamy, at least 4 hours or preferably overnight. Give it a good stir before serving and enjoy cold.

Rose-Mango Rice Pudding

Serves 8 | Active Time: 30 minutes | Total Time: 45 minutes

The main difference between traditional rice pudding and this Lebanese version, which we call riz bi haleeb, *is the use of rose water to add a subtle hint of floral flavor. And because I love making things a little extra without adding any effort, I simmer this rice pudding with mango chunks. The resulting dessert is somehow both decadent and refreshing. Whether you prefer your rice pudding chilled or warm, I cannot tell you how satisfying it is to dig in. By the way, the ratio of one cup of rice to nine cups of milk is not a typo. Here, the rice puffs and almost melts into the liquid, creating an absolutely perfect rice pudding texture.*

1 cup short-grain rice
(do not rinse)

9 cups whole milk, divided

¾ cup granulated sugar

1 tablespoon cornstarch

2 cups mango chunks
(fresh or frozen)

4 teaspoons rose water

1 teaspoon vanilla extract

⅛ teaspoon salt

1. In a large pot, add the rice and 1 cup of water. Bring to a boil over medium-high heat and cook, stirring occasionally, until the water is mostly absorbed, 3 to 5 minutes.

2. Add 8 cups of the milk and the sugar to the pot. Bring everything to a rapid simmer and then reduce the heat to medium-low. Cook, stirring frequently, until the rice is tender and the milk begins to thicken, about 15 minutes.

3. Dissolve the cornstarch in the remaining 1 cup of milk. Stir the cornstarch-milk mixture into the pot, then stir in the mango, rose water, vanilla, and salt. Continue to cook, stirring a few times throughout, until the rice is extremely plump and the mixture is thickened and very creamy, 30 to 35 minutes longer.

4. Serve the rice pudding warm or chilled in individual serving bowls.

Raspberry Rose Fro-Yo

Makes about 2 pints | Active Time: 10 minutes | Total Time: 10 minutes (plus freezing)

Okay, I cannot be humble about this fro-yo recipe. It's just too good! It's just too beautiful! It's only four ingredients, and it has the perfect texture without the use of an ice-cream maker. The soft pink color is also pretty special. All you do is blend up frozen raspberries, whole-milk Greek yogurt (using full fat is important here), and just the right amount of floral rose water with a can of sweetened condensed milk for one of the easiest, most elegant homemade desserts of all time.

2 cups frozen raspberries

2 cups whole-milk Greek yogurt

1 (14-ounce) can sweetened condensed milk

1 tablespoon rose water

⅛ teaspoon salt

1. In a food processor, add the raspberries, yogurt, condensed milk, rose water, and salt. Process, scraping down the sides as needed, until extremely smooth, about 2 minutes.

2. Transfer the fro-yo to a storage container and freeze, tightly sealed, until firm, at least 4 hours and up to 1 month. Let thaw for 5 minutes at room temperature before scooping and serving.

Three-Ingredient Mango Sorbet

Makes about 2 pints | Active Time: 10 minutes | Total Time: 10 minutes

Blend frozen mango, maple syrup, and lime in a food processor and you have the most gorgeous sunshine-colored mango soft serve. I love enjoying it right away, but just as often I like to pop it in the freezer to chill overnight, which gives it a more sorbet-like texture. Seriously, this dessert tastes like biting into a fresh, ripe mango. So good!

5 cups (about 20 ounces) frozen mango chunks

2 limes

⅓ cup maple syrup

⅛ teaspoon salt

1. Pulse the mango in a food processor, scraping down the sides as needed, until the mango is chopped into pea-size pieces.

2. Zest one of the limes into the food processor. Add the juice of both limes, the maple syrup, and salt. Continue processing until extremely smooth and creamy, about 1 minute.

3. Enjoy immediately or transfer to a storage container and freeze, tightly sealed, for up to 1 month. Let thaw for 5 minutes at room temperature before scooping and serving.

Pistachio & Coconut Yogurt Ice Pops

Makes 6 ice pops   Active Time: 10 minutes   Total Time: 10 minutes (plus freezing)

My kids love a simple frozen dessert in the afternoon or at the end of the day—and I love that I can blend up yogurt with a few ingredients and call it a treat. These fresh coconutty ice pops satisfy their sweet tooth without being over-the-top indulgent, with a creamy texture, chewy shredded coconut, and nutty pistachios. If you don't have ice pop molds, feel free to use one of the old nineties tricks of the trade: sticks plus a deep ice cube tray or small paper cups!

1¾ cups coconut yogurt

Zest and juice of 1 lime

⅓ cup maple syrup

⅛ teaspoon salt

2 tablespoons unsweetened shredded coconut

3 tablespoons finely chopped shelled pistachios

1. In a medium bowl, whisk the yogurt, lime zest, lime juice, maple syrup, and salt until smooth. Fold in the coconut.

2. Pour the yogurt mixture into six 3-ounce ice pop molds. Evenly sprinkle the exposed part of the yogurt mixture (what will become the bottom of the ice pop) with the pistachios.

3. Insert the sticks and freeze for at least 6 hours or overnight. Unmold and enjoy! Store the ice pops in the freezer for up to 1 month.

Mixed Berry Sumac Crisp

Serves 8   Active Time: 10 minutes   Total Time: 50 minutes

I turn to berry crisp whenever I have extra berries on hand that are getting a little too ripe. What makes this crisp extra special is a hint of sumac in the filling and rich, nutty tahini in the topping. The sumac is tart and bright like lemon juice but doesn't add any liquid. The tahini works like butter but carries the most delicious, subtle sesame flavor. And the best thing about this recipe, really, is how versatile it is: feel free to use frozen mixed berries instead of fresh or to substitute five cups of diced apples or peaches. The finished dessert is wonderful on its own but also delicious with a scoop of vanilla ice cream on top.

Filling

5 cups (about 20 ounces) **mixed berries** (fresh or frozen)

2 tablespoons all-purpose flour

2 tablespoons granulated sugar

2 teaspoons ground sumac

Topping

¾ cup rolled oats

¾ cup all-purpose flour

½ cup (packed) **light brown sugar**

1 teaspoon ground cinnamon

Salt

½ cup tahini

Ice cream, for serving (optional)

1. Preheat the oven to 375°F.

2. Add the berries to an 8 × 8-inch baking dish. Sprinkle the flour, granulated sugar, and sumac on top and stir to incorporate. Set aside.

3. In a medium bowl, combine the oats, flour, brown sugar, cinnamon, and a pinch of salt. Add the tahini on top. Using a fork, stir and distribute the tahini into the oat mixture until it resembles coarse crumbs. Sprinkle the crumb topping evenly over the filling.

4. Bake until the topping is golden brown and the filling is bubbly, 35 to 40 minutes. Let cool for 5 minutes before serving warm with a scoop of ice cream (if using).

No-Bake Walnut Cheesecake

Serves 12   Active Time: 30 minutes   Total Time: 30 minutes (plus chilling)

Easy no-bake cheesecake is the unsung hero of the cheesecake world. Here, the cream cheese filling is light, airy, and mousse-like, and the pressed walnut crust has just the right amount of sweetness and spice. It's also naturally gluten-free, which is always nice when feeding a crowd that might have different sensitivities. For clean, even cuts when serving, remember to wipe the knife clean with a warm, damp kitchen towel in between each slice. I think you'll love the results as much as I do.

Crust

2 cups unsalted raw walnuts

⅓ cup granulated sugar

1¼ teaspoons ground cardamom

¼ teaspoon salt

¼ cup (½ stick) **unsalted butter,** melted

Filling

2 cups heavy cream, divided

2 (8-ounce) **packages cream cheese,** at room temperature

½ cup granulated sugar

1 teaspoon vanilla extract

Fresh berries, for serving

1. Line a 9-inch round springform pan with parchment paper, making sure that the bottom and sides are evenly covered. Set aside.

2. To make the crust, pulse the walnuts, sugar, cardamom, and salt in a food processor until very finely chopped. Pour in the butter and pulse until everything is incorporated. It should hold together easily when pinched between two fingers without being too crumbly or too wet and sticky.

3. Evenly press the walnut crust on the bottom and slightly up the sides of the prepared pan—use your fingers or the flat bottom of a glass to tightly pack the crust in a single layer. Chill the crust in the fridge while you make the filling.

4. Using an electric hand mixer on medium-high speed, whip ½ cup of the heavy cream with the cream cheese, sugar, and vanilla in a medium bowl until incorporated and smooth, about 2 minutes.

5. In a separate medium bowl, whip the remaining 1½ cups of heavy cream on medium-high speed until it forms stiff peaks. Fold about one-third of the whipped cream into the cream cheese mixture to lighten it. Using the electric hand mixer on low speed, beat the remaining whipped cream into the cream cheese mixture until no lumps remain.

6. Pour the filling into the prepared crust. Use the back of a spoon to smooth out the surface of the filling. Tightly cover and refrigerate the cheesecake for at least 12 hours before slicing and topping with berries.

Citrus & Turmeric Cake

Serves 16 to 20 | Active Time: 20 minutes | Total Time: 50 minutes

I used sfouf—a bright yellow Lebanese cake with turmeric and semolina flour—as the inspiration for this citrusy, Midwestern-style tea cake. This recipe is the perfect hybrid of my Middle Eastern and Michiganian roots! Listen: It was tested eleven times, and the labor of love was so, so worth it! The color and flavors are amazing, and having a thick slice with tea is seriously one of my favorite treats. Semolina has wonderful texture and hearty crumb, but if you can't find it, don't worry—you can just replace it with more all-purpose flour. This recipe uses a key technique for infusing flavor: rubbing citrus zest into sugar until the sugar starts to take on the color of the zest. By infusing the sugar with the essential oils of the citrus, you're really getting the most out of your ingredients flavorwise. Plus, it's such a satisfying process.

1½ cups all-purpose flour

¼ cup semolina flour

1 tablespoon ground turmeric

1 teaspoon baking powder

⅛ teaspoon salt

1 orange

1 lemon

1 cup granulated sugar

2 large eggs

1 cup whole-milk Greek yogurt

½ cup (1 stick) **unsalted butter,** melted and slightly cooled

1 teaspoon vanilla extract

1. Preheat the oven to 350°F. Line an 8 × 8-inch baking dish with parchment paper, leaving about 2 inches of extra parchment over both sides.

2. In a medium bowl, whisk the all-purpose flour, semolina flour, turmeric, baking powder, and salt and set aside.

3. Zest 1 tablespoon each from the orange and lemon into a large bowl, reserving the rest of the citrus for later. Add the sugar to the bowl with the zest. Using your fingertips, rub the zest into the sugar until fragrant and starting to take on the color of the zest.

4. Whisk the eggs into the sugar until smooth, then whisk in the yogurt, butter, and vanilla. Juice about half of the lemon and orange for a total of ¼ cup of citrus juice, and then whisk that in, too.

5. Fold the dry ingredients into the wet until no streaks of flour remain. Pour the batter into the prepared pan and smooth over the top.

6. Bake until the edges are lightly browned and a toothpick inserted in the center comes out clean, 33 to 38 minutes. Let cool in the pan for 10 minutes, then transfer to a wire rack to cool completely. Slice into 16 squares or about 20 diamonds.

Whipped Ricotta & Honey-Glazed Peaches

Serves 4   Active Time: 15 minutes   Total Time: 35 minutes

Forget about whipped cream—today you're whipping ricotta! Ricotta is such a versatile ingredient in both sweet and savory recipes, so I always tend to have it in my fridge. Whipped ricotta is light and airy like whipped cream but has a unique, velvety texture that's so good dolloped on top of fresh peaches glazed in honey. If you can't find ripe peaches or if it's just not the season for stone fruit, try pears instead.

3 tablespoons honey, plus more for serving

2 tablespoons extra-virgin olive oil, divided

4 peaches, pitted and quartered

1 cup whole-milk ricotta

Salt

1. Preheat the oven to 400°F. Line a baking sheet with parchment paper.

2. In a small bowl, mix the honey with 1 tablespoon of the oil. Place the peaches cut side down on the prepared baking sheet, and brush the honey mixture all over the peaches. Roast until browned and caramelized, 25 to 28 minutes. Divide the peaches between four individual serving bowls and set aside to cool.

3. Meanwhile, in a food processor, pulse the ricotta and salt to combine. With the motor running, slowly stream in the remaining 1 tablespoon of oil. Process until the ricotta is whipped and airy, about 1 minute.

4. Dollop a generous spoonful of whipped ricotta on top of the peaches and finish with a drizzle of honey.

Banana Tahini Shake

Serves 2 | Active Time: 5 minutes | Total Time: 5 minutes

What's the difference between a smoothie and a shake? Context! I prefer my milkshakes thicker, richer, and creamier with milk—I use whole or 2 percent, but use whatever milk you like, including plant-based. I also make my shakes slightly sweeter because even though I'm choosing to add some nutrient-packed ingredients like bananas and tahini, it's still a dessert taste I'm after! Trust me, this frosty drink is the perfect treat any time of day.

2 frozen bananas

¼ cup tahini

5 ice cubes

1 tablespoon maple syrup

½ teaspoon ground cinnamon

1½ cups milk of choice

In a blender, add the bananas, tahini, ice cubes, maple syrup, cinnamon, and milk. Blend on high speed until smooth, thick, and creamy, 30 to 60 seconds. Enjoy immediately.

Mint-Basil Lemonade

Makes about 6 cups | Active Time: 10 minutes | Total Time: 10 minutes

This homemade lemonade is refreshing, hydrating, and bright green with fresh mint and basil. It's just sweet enough, packed with vitamin C, and truly special despite its simplicity. There's no need to strain the lemonade after blending if you have a high-speed blender—but if you don't, just pour the drink through a fine-mesh sieve before storing for a nice, smooth texture.

6 lemons

⅓ cup honey

¼ cup fresh mint leaves

¼ cup fresh basil leaves

Zest 2 of the lemons into a high-speed blender. Add the juice of all 6 lemons (about 1 cup), the honey, mint, basil, and 4 cups of cold water. Blend until the mixture is completely smooth and bright green, 30 to 40 seconds. Transfer to three glass pint jars and store, tightly sealed, in the fridge for up to 4 days. When ready to serve, shake vigorously and pour in a glass over ice.

Whipped Coffee

Serves 2 | Active Time: 10 minutes | Total Time: 10 minutes

Whipped coffee—also called dalgona coffee—was all the rage during the early weeks of the pandemic. It resonated with me, especially, because in Lebanon, if we're not making Turkish-style coffee on the stovetop, we're enjoying instant coffee mixed with hot water. Since I already had instant coffee in my pantry, I was one of the first people to make and post this recipe in the States, and let me tell you, social media soon exploded with viral videos of latte-colored clouds. This recipe is now the most popular beverage on my website, and it's well loved for a reason: making whipped coffee at home couldn't be simpler, even though it looks fancy enough for a coffee shop.

2 tablespoons instant coffee

2 tablespoons granulated sugar

2 tablespoons boiling water

2 cups milk of choice

1. In a small bowl, add the instant coffee, sugar, and boiling water. Using a milk frother or an electric hand mixer fitted with the whisk attachment on medium-high speed, whisk until you have thick, soft peaks of latte-colored coffee, 5 to 8 minutes.

2. Divide the milk between two cups. Add ice if you're serving it cold. Evenly spoon the whipped coffee over the milk and serve.

Rose Latte

Serves 2 | Active Time: 5 minutes | Total Time: 5 minutes

When I want to take my latte to the next level, a floral dash of rose water always hits the spot! I use the recipe below when I'm making coffee for two, but for a solo drink, here's my trick: Halve the ingredient amounts, skip the saucepan, pour the milk into a deep mug, and warm the milk in the microwave with the sugar and rose water before frothing with a handheld milk frother. Then pour in your espresso and stir!

1½ cups milk

2 teaspoons granulated sugar

1 teaspoon rose water

1 cup hot brewed espresso or strong coffee

Dried edible rose petals, for garnish (optional)

1. Heat the milk in a small saucepan over medium heat, stirring frequently. Add the sugar and rose water. Stir until the sugar is dissolved.

2. Using a handheld frother (or a whisk and some elbow grease), whisk the milk in the saucepan until frothy. Evenly divide the espresso between two mugs and then divide the rose milk on top. Garnish with rose petals (if using).

Acknowledgments

The Feel Good Foodie community: Some of you have been there from day one. Many of you have watched my baby blog grow and my own babies grow over the past eleven years. I used to think that there were too many recipes on the Internet and I had nothing new to add. Thank you for showing me that there is space for me and my recipes with your interest, encouragement, and endless support. This book is for the thousands of DMs I've received from you all over the years asking if I have a cookbook. I hope you enjoy it!

Mama & Baba: From the delicious meals you prepared for our family to the invaluable lessons you taught me in the kitchen, you have instilled in me a deep appreciation for food and its ability to bring people together. Your love, guidance, and sacrifices have shaped me into the strong Lebanese American woman I am today. Thank you for being the foundation of my skills, my creativity, and my identity.

Janis: Thank you for not taking no for an answer the first four times you asked me to write a cookbook. You were right that busy people write better books.

Dervla: I knew from the first time we chatted ten months before I even wrote a cookbook proposal that you were the editor I wanted to work with. Your insightful feedback, brilliant guidance, and invaluable support have made this process as smooth as butter. We've created a gorgeous cookbook together, and I'm incredibly grateful for this opportunity!

Stephanie, Katherine, Kim, Michelle, Bridget, and the Penguin team: You're the dream team that any author would be so fortunate to work with.

Julia: I'm not as good with words as you are, but thank you for getting in my head somehow and sharing my stories about these recipes better than I could have imagined. We ate a lot of oatmeal chocolate chip cookies and citrus and turmeric cake in the process of perfecting the recipes and narrative, and I appreciate your meticulousness and attention to detail every step of the way.

Rawan: I'm so lucky to have you by my side on recipe testing days to validate my craziness when I think a recipe needs to be tested for the seventh time. I've learned so many culinary skills and tips working with you. You are so genuine in your feedback, creative with your solutions, and a joy to work with!

Doaa: It amazes me how you create the most stunning scenes and compelling stories through your photography. Your talents are awe-inspiring, and your compassion shines through in every shot. Thank you for capturing the recipes better than I could have imagined!

Olivia and Charlotte: You both bring effortless energy to every set. It was so inspiring to watch you both cook and style 125 recipes in eleven days with such ease and confidence. You brought these recipes to life with your expertise, creativity, and passion, and you never settled for anything less than perfect, even it meant remaking recipes or swapping surfaces for the perfect shot.

Helena: You have such a way of styling my home for the cookbook and for real life that makes it look so effortless and personable.

Danya: Thank you for styling me to express my brand and personality! You bring a new meaning to "Look good, feel good."

Kristina and Rosana: I loved watching you both so passionately cook my cookbook recipes with so much dedication and attention to detail!

Julie: Thank you for your help in rigorously cross-testing the recipes to make sure they worked flawlessly. I appreciate your extra set of hands and whisks!

Aiman, Rawan, and Zainab: We grew up so fortunate to have Mama's and Baba's grace, guidance, and good food! I hope I've captured the good food part in this cookbook so we can keep it in our family for generations to come. And I hope you know how much your love and support mean to me!

My girlfriends (you know who you are): Thanks for being my taste testers, my board of advisors, and my cheerleaders.

My mother-in-law, Salwa: You were so proud of this cookbook that you even tested a few of the recipes early on and added some to your dinner rotations! Your sincerity, compassion, and love make me feel so blessed.

Carine and Adam: Your curiosity, creativity, and willingness to explore new tastes and textures in the kitchen continue to amaze me. You have both become my trusted sous chefs, and I cherish our time cooking together. Thank you for being my constant source of inspiration, motivation, and joy.

Wassim: I love that you pushed me to create Feel Good Foodie (and even came up with the name!). Our families call us the pot and lid, and I'd be lost and laughing less without you.

Index

Note: Page references in *italics* indicate photographs.

M

N

O

About the Author

Yumna Jawad is an entrepreneur, social media influencer, and recipe developer. She is the founder of the popular Feel Good Foodie website dedicated to healthy-ish recipes with feel-good ingredients, and she is the founder of the packaged overnight oats brand Oath. A graduate of the University of Michigan business school, she has created a massive social media following from her viral food trends and videos, with millions of followers on multiple platforms. She lives in Grand Rapids, Michigan, with her husband and two kids.